Evil In Town

Vol 1

*5 Most Disturbing Crime Stories Of
Murder, Heists And Deception*

Zara Sinclair

Disclaimer

The information contained in this book is based on extensive research and diligent efforts to provide accurate and reliable accounts of true crime events. However, the author and publisher make no representations or warranties of any kind, express or implied, about the completeness, accuracy, reliability, suitability, or availability of the information contained herein.

The content of this book is intended for informational purposes only and should not be considered as professional advice or a substitute for consultation with experts in the field. The reader is solely responsible for any actions or decisions made based on the information presented in this book.

Table Of Contents

Case 1

The Woman Scorned

Laurel Fair, originally known as Laura Hall, was born in Holly Springs, Mississippi, on June 22, 1837. At the age of 16, she entered into her first marriage, and by 1863, she had been married three times, widowed twice, and was supporting her young daughter. During this time, she owned and managed a hotel in Virginia City, Nevada, just as the Comstock Lode was bringing wealth to the region.

It was during this period that Alexander Crittenden entered Laurel's life. Crittenden, a 47-year-old San Francisco lawyer, graduate of West Point, and former California state legislator, arrived in Virginia City with the intention of establishing a law practice and capitalizing on the prosperity brought by the silver industry. He took up residence at the Tahoe House, Laurel's hotel,Sure! Here's a paraphrased version of the passage you provided:

Laurel Fair was born as Laura Hall in Holly Spring, Mississippi on June 22, 1837. At the age of 16, she got married for the first time, and by 1863, she had been married three times and widowed twice. During this time, she owned and operated a hotel in Virginia City, Nevada, just as the Comstock Lode was leading to substantial wealth for some individuals.

It was during this period that Alexander Crittenden entered her life. Crittenden, a 47-year-old lawyer from San Francisco and a former member of the California state legislature, had graduated from West Point. He came to Virginia City to establish a law practice and hoped to benefit from the prosperity brought about by the silver industry. Upon his arrival, he settled in the Tahoe House, which was Laurel's hotel. By the end of 1863, the prosperous lawyer and the successful hotel owner became romantically involved, professing their love for each other and discussing marriage.

Unfortunately, and perhaps unbeknownst to Laurel, Crittenden was already married, a fact he had apparently failed to mention. Adding to Crittenden's misfortune, his eldest son, married and with a pregnant daughter, along with his legally wedded wife, arrived in Virginia City in early 1864 to reside with him. The truth was revealed, and Crittenden managed to weather the storm by assuring Laurel that he would divorce his wife and marry her, though it would take some time. Five years later, Crittenden returned to San Francisco and resumed his life with his wife and family, while still maintaining a relationship with Fair, who had followed him to the Bay Area.

During their relationship, Crittenden also sent Fair to Indiana briefly, claiming that the divorce laws there were more lenient. He promised to join her there, but he never showed up. By 1870, Fair had reached her limit and reportedly even fired a shot at Crittenden during an argument.

Seeking solace, she married a man named Jesse Snyder, which greatly upset Crittenden. In a letter to Fair about her marriage, he expressed his wretchedness and inability to focus on anything but her.

The two eventually reconciled and made promises to divorce their respective spouses. Fair followed through with her promise, but Crittenden did not.

Murder

Around that time, something within Laura Fair snapped. She exchanged her Colt revolver, which she had used to take a shot at Crittenden, for a four-barrel Sharps derringer. She dressed entirely in black, including a black veil, and trailed Crittenden to the railroad station in Oakland. There, she witnessed Clara's return from the East and what seemed to be a tender reunion between her and her husband.

Fair continued to follow the couple, accompanied by three of their seven children who had come to greet their mother, as they boarded the El Capitan, a side-wheel steamer bound for San Francisco. Concealed by her veil, she took a seat where she could observe them. Finally, just as the ferry was departing, she rose from her seat and approached Crittenden, who also stood up. She shot him once in the chest, dropped the derringer, and walked away.

Crittenden's 14-year-old son, Parker, and a police officer who happened to be on the ferry pursued Fair and confronted her in the wheelhouse. According to reports, she admitted to the act by saying, "I did it. I don't deny it. He has ruined me and my child, and I meant to kill him." In that regard, she had succeeded. Crittenden was taken to his home in San Francisco and survived for another 48 hours before succumbing to his injuries.

The era of the "lawless frontier," though it was never entirely lawless, was coming to an end. By 1870, the West was undergoing changes, as Laura Fair would soon discover firsthand. She was accustomed to being a woman in a male-dominated West and getting her way as a result. However, Laura was in for a surprise. The

West was evolving, and she found herself charged with murder.

The handling of Laura's case was delayed due to jurisdictional concerns. The shooting occurred aboard the El Capitan, which was traveling between Alameda County and San Francisco County, making it initially unclear in which county the incident had taken place. A survey of the harbor was required to establish that Crittenden had met his fate in San Francisco County.

Consequently, it took five months before Fair went on trial in the San Francisco County Courthouse. The trial, as one historian described it, "became a national sensation. It captured the fears of adulterous men everywhere and garnered sympathy from women's rights activists." Additionally, a contemporary historian characterized it as a "ritualized dramatic enactment of the community's moral values."

But what were those moral values? For suffragettes and early feminists who packed the courtroom, the trial symbolized the double standard that, according to them, governed Victorian morality. This double standard turned a blind eye to men having affairs while considering adulterous women as home-wrecking villains. For the respectable citizens of San Francisco, it represented the intrusion of an "evil siren" who had shattered a harmonious family. One newspaper even labeled her as a "saucy wench." On a broader scale, the trial represented the establishment of order and law in the West as a whole.

Case 2

The Train Wrecker

Szilveszter Matuska, a Serbian-born engineer, gained infamy during the early 1930s for his involvement in train wrecks in Hungary and Austria. Over a two-year period, he engineered four train derailments, resulting in the deaths of 22 people and numerous injuries. Matuska admitted to enjoying witnessing the crashes and experiencing sexual pleasure from the destruction. The motivations behind his actions remain unclear to this day, leading to speculation about whether he was politically motivated, mentally disturbed, or had other motives altogether. While there were suspicions of his involvement with communism due to anti-Nazi graffiti found at one crash site and rumors of connections to Russian and Chinese military efforts, the true reasons behind his actions remain elusive. After his capture, Matuska escaped from a Hungarian prison during World War II and disappeared. Various rumors surround his later life and fate, but they lack substantiation. The story of Szilveszter Matuska is clouded with uncertainty and speculation, leaving his true motivations and ultimate destiny unanswered.

Case 3

The Dog That Stood Trial for Murder

San Francisco has had its fair share of notorious murderers throughout the years, including the Zodiac and the Night Stalker. In the early 1970s, the city was the epicenter of the infamous "Zebra" killings, and Charles Manson, before becoming a symbol of evil, spent time in Haight-Ashbury in 1967. Another killer, though of a different kind, made headlines during the Roaring Twenties in the City by the Bay. This particular killer carried out his gruesome acts in broad daylight, enjoyed gnawing on bones, and was entirely covered in hair. His name was Dormie, the Airedale Terrier, and he was infamous for killing cats in San Francisco.

When Dormie was finally apprehended, he didn't end up in a local animal shelter. Instead, he found himself in a California courtroom, facing a judge and a jury of twelve human peers. Over the following days, these jurors would determine whether Dormie would live to see another day or be put down.

The story begins in 1921, the same year when Hollywood superstar Roscoe "Fatty" Arbuckle stood trial for the death of actress Virginia Rappe. On an ordinary December day, Sunbeam, a Persian-Angora cat, was peacefully relaxing in her backyard, caring for her kittens. Mrs. Marjorie Ingals, Sunbeam's owner, happened to look outside and witnessed a brown, black, and furry creature darting under the fence and heading straight for Sunbeam's kittens. In a matter of moments, the dog attacked and killed three of Sunbeam's kittens before turning its attention to the mother. Mrs. Ingals described how the dog clamped its jaws around Sunbeam's neck, shook her violently, and then discarded her battered body on the ground. This attack was just one of many cat killings attributed to Dormie, who had claimed the lives of fourteen victims.

Marjorie Ingals, harboring a grudge against Dormie's owner, Eaton McMillan, took action. McMillan, a wealthy car dealer, faced an ultimatum at a neighborhood meeting: either have Dormie euthanized or face legal consequences. When McMillan refused to put his dog down, he was charged with a misdemeanor. In the 1920s, if you owned a "dangerous or vicious" dog, you could be fined, and your dog would be put to sleep. However, McMillan refused to pay the fine, arguing that he had purchased a license for Dormie, which allowed the terrier to roam freely in San Francisco without being held accountable for its actions. McMillan also claimed that he never encouraged Dormie to kill cats.

Instead of abandoning Dormie to the California legal system, McMillan hired defense lawyer James F. Brennan. The case ended up in Police Judge Lile T. Jack's courtroom, where Brennan requested a trial by jury. This marked the beginning of one of the most extraordinary cases in American legal history.

While the idea of a dog standing trial may seem absurd, it was not entirely uncommon in world history. During the Middle Ages, animals were often held responsible for breaking human laws, regardless of their fur, feathers, or scales. Animal trials were prevalent in Europe from 824 A.D. to the 1700s, with dogs, horses, and even eels being brought into court. More often than not, these animals were sentenced to death. For instance, in 1314, a bull was hanged for murder, and in 1474, a rooster was burned for supposedly laying an egg, considered a bizarre occurrence. Surprisingly, in 1595, three dolphins were sentenced to death in Marseilles, although the reasons and methods of their execution remain unknown.During the Middle Ages, various animals frequently found themselves in legal trouble, but pigs were the primary offenders. This was likely due to the abundance of pigs during that time, as well as their indiscriminate eating habits. In 1379, three troublesome pigs were responsible for the death of a French farmer, while their fellow four-legged companions encouraged them with cries and aggressive behavior. All the pigs were brought to court, but their owner managed to persuade the Duke of Burgundy to pardon the onlookers.

In 1386, an even stranger incident occurred in the town of Falaise, France. After devouring a baby, the guilty pig was dressed in human attire, including gloves, pants, and a face mask. The unfortunate swine was swiftly tried and subsequently hanged until dead.

Not all pigs met a grim fate, though. In 1547, a sow and her piglets were charged with "murdering" a young boy. While the mother was hanged from a tree by her hind legs, the piglets were released due to their youth and the corrupting influence of their mother.

Donkeys also occasionally escaped execution. In 1750, a jackass was accused of bestiality, but after a compassionate witness testified to the animal's virtuous nature, the court decided to set the poor creature free. However, the offending human involved wasn't as fortunate.

There was an even worse fate than execution, though. If an animal ended up in an ecclesiastical court governed by church officials, it could face excommunication, a punishment believed to bring divine retribution. One of the most famous cases of animal excommunication occurred in 16th century France when a group of rats in the Autun province was charged with feloniously consuming a barley crop. If found guilty, they would be cut off from God's grace.

Fortunately for the rodents, they had a skilled advocate in Bartholomew Chassenee, akin to the renowned lawyer Clarence Darrow of the time. Determined to spare the rats from eternal damnation, Bartholomew employed a clever legal argument. He contended that the court couldn't excommunicate the rats without first summoning them to appear. However, summoning all the rats was nearly impossible, and if they left their hiding places, they risked being hunted by hungry cats.

Remarkably, the judge agreed with Bartholomew's argument, and the case was dismissed.

So, what motivated people to prosecute their pets and livestock? Was it to assert human dominance over the animal kingdom? Was it merely a pastime for medieval lawyers? Or perhaps it served as a means of coping with the hardships of everyday life. When something unfortunate occurred, people sought justice, and sometimes animals became scapegoats, quite literally. Perhaps that is why, many years later, Marjorie Ingals decided to take Dormie to court.

Dormie was responsible for the death of her beloved pet, and she believed he should face the consequences. Whatever the motive behind it, whether it was revenge or simple jealousy, the 1921 Airedale trial was part of a peculiar and longstanding tradition. However, unlike their European ancestors who took such cases seriously, most residents of San Francisco found Dormie's trial to be comical.

When Dormie's representative, James F. Brennan, demanded a jury trial for his furry client, it came as a surprise to Assistant District Attorney John Orcutt, who assumed the case was straightforward. After all, there were 16 witnesses ready to testify, and it was just a dog, for crying out loud. However, Brennan was determined. He insisted on a trial by jury, with a panel consisting entirely of dogs.

Orcutt had his limits with such absurdity and responded by stating that most dogs were better than people. Since Dormie was clearly a troublemaker, Orcutt believed he should be judged by 12 human beings.

The trial took place on December 21, 1921, and the courtroom was packed. Dormie was a popular dog in the town, and numerous children attended the proceedings. The children were so invested in Dormie's case that they even collected money to cover his legal expenses.

Brennan's initial strategy was to undermine the credibility of the prosecution's main witness, Marjorie Ingals. Hoping to demonstrate that Mrs. Ingals was unreliable in identifying dogs, Brennan brought various neighborhood dogs into the courtroom and asked her to identify the assailant of her pet, Sunbeam. He presented a water spaniel, a mastiff, a Russian wolfhound, and several Airedales, including Dormie's brother.

Brennan's plan backfired slightly when Mrs. Ingals correctly identified Dormie. However, Brennan promptly pointed out that Dormie had been escorted into the courtroom by a police officer. Judge Jacks acknowledged this point and instructed the jurors to disregard the lineup entirely.

After questioning Mrs. Ingals about whether Sunbeam had provoked the attack, Brennan called his first character witness, Rowdy. Rowdy was another Airedale Terrier and happened to be the brother of President Warren G. Harding's pet. Brennan revealed that Rowdy was best friends with a Persian cat named Mary Ann and supposedly mourned for eight days after the cat passed away. This testimony aimed to show that Airedales were not vicious towards cats.

As one might imagine, the newspapers had a field day with Dormie's trial. The Chicago Tribune reported that Dormie was "being persecuted by the sausage trust," being sued by a female dog for "breach of promise," and causing consternation in the fashionable Burlingame kennels by threatening to expose the inner secrets of dogdom's upper hierarchy. Dormie was also quoted as describing San Francisco's cat population as "exceedingly catty."There was a particular reporter whoOne reporter in particular seemed to thoroughly enjoy his job. However, not everyone shared the same sentiment regarding Dormie's trial. On January 21, 1922, The Washington Times published a letter from a concerned citizen named Harold A. Israel. Mr. Israel argued that the purpose of a trial was to deter future criminals from committing crimes. However, he astutely pointed out that "executing a dog can serve no such purpose." Whether Dormie was found innocent or guilty, according to Mr. Israel, it would not prevent other dogs from behaving like dogs and chasing cats.

It appears that most of the jurors agreed with Mr. Israel. After deliberating on the case, eleven jurors voted to set Dormie free, while only one believed he should be euthanized. The result was a hung jury. Capitalizing on this opportunity, James Brennan requested that the court dismiss the case, and not surprisingly, Judge Jacks agreed. Not only did the judge dismiss the case, but he also invalidated the law that imposed the death penalty for "vicious and dangerous" dogs. Judge Jacks expressed that licensed dogs were free to go wherever they pleased, and cats simply needed to avoid their path.

Perhaps Judge Jacks had his own Airedale at home.

Unfortunately, the fate of Dormie following the trial remains unknown. Did he resume his predatory behavior, or did he become a law-abiding member of the canine community? We may never find out. However, while the Airedale trial may seem like a big joke, it could potentially have significant implications for future cases involving dangerous dogs.

In an article for Psychology Today, Professor Stanley Corner of the University of British Columbia suggests that Dormie's trial may have established several unique legal precedents. Most notably, dogs now have the right to a trial by jury. The case also implies that dogs can present character witnesses, challenge death penalties for dogs, and that cats have no legal rights whatsoever.

While it may sound like a prank, legal cases often rely on previous decisions as references. It is possible that someday a lawyer might refer back to the Dormie trial of 1921 to argue for the acquittal of another potentially dangerous dog. In other words, it would be wise to keep your cats indoors.

Case 4

Beauty, Wealth and a Dead Bride

The locations had captivating names: Gugulethu, Lingelethu, Khayelitsha, Chitwa Chitwa. They evoked images of vibrant people dancing to the rhythm of drums on a sultry summer night.

However, to the police officers in their somber blue uniforms gathered around the abandoned white Volkswagen Sharan in Lingelethu, there was nothing exotic about the lifeless young woman sprawled across the car's rear seat. The two bullet holes between her shoulders and another in her neck, from which blood had freely flowed, covering most of the car's interior, made it clear to them that she was dead.

They knew her name: Anni Dewani.

The officers pondered how they were going to break the news to her husband, Shrien, who had reported her missing in the early hours of that morning and anxiously awaited updates at a nearby luxury hotel.

It was a Sunday, November 13, 2010, shortly after 7 a.m. The day had already dawned two hours earlier, as is the norm in Africa, where the sun rises early and darkness falls swiftly.

To be precise, it was South Africa—a country that had recently emerged from three centuries of institutionalized racial segregation, known as apartheid, to attain freedom and happiness. However, it struggled with a crime rate that had become one of the highest in the developing world. Statistics released by the South African government in September 2010 revealed alarming figures: a total of 2,121,887 serious crimes had been committed between April 2009 and March 2010. Among these were 68,332 cases of rape, 17,410 attempted murders, 16,834 murders, 14,542 instances of illegal firearm possession, 13,902 carjackings, 2,889 kidnappings, and 256,577 residential burglaries.

Given these circumstances, the officers surrounding the Sharan could be described as hardened, yet even they found it difficult to swallow the reality before them.

Anni and Shrien Dewani were tourists from England. They were on their honeymoon. After enjoying a safari in the northern part of the country, they had traveled south and checked into the luxurious five-star hotel, The Cape Grace, located in Cape Town, South Africa's parliamentary capital.

The couple seemingly had everything to live for, yet now one of them lay lifeless, a victim of murder.

The previous night, nearing midnight, Shrien Dewani, a 30-year-old handsome Anglo-Indian millionaire from Bristol, England, had approached the hotel's receptionist in distress. He reported that a taxi carrying him and his wife had been hijacked by two armed men who had driven off with Anni, his 28-year-old wife.

Upon hearing this, the police swiftly responded to the hotel. It was not the time to speak of luck, so they refrained from informing Dewani that he was fortunate to have survived. In carjacking incidents, the fate of the passengers almost always involved death.

They also chose not to reveal the grim likelihood of his wife being raped by the assailants—there was a 99.99 percent chance of it happening—followed by her murder, either by gunshot or knife.

How it had happened

Dewani provided his account to the police. According to him, on the previous night at 8:30, a taxi had arrived at the hotel to take him and his wife to a restaurant in the upscale beach resort of The Strand, located 31 miles southeast of Cape Town.

He explained that because Anni wanted to experience authentic African culture, they had requested the driver, a man named Zola Tongo, to take them through one of the residential areas surrounding Cape Town where Black African people reside. These areas are referred to as townships. During the apartheid era, only white Europeans were permitted to live in the cities and towns, while Black Africans, as well as people of mixed race and Asian descent, were legally required to live in townships or locations. Although apartheid officially ended in 1994, a combination of housing shortages and poverty has prevented these ethnic groups from relocating to the previously all-white urban areas.

Life in a township is marked by insecurity and squalor. The residents live in shacks without electricity, hot water, or heating during the winter. However, townships have become tourist attractions because affluent foreigners believe that they offer an opportunity to experience the "real Africa." Visitors can indulge in African cuisine cooked in traditional iron pots over open fires, enjoy frothy African beer, and dance to vibrant African music all night long.

Gugulethu, Lingelethu, and Khayelitsha were examples of such townships, located in close proximity to Cape Town. Gugulethu, situated 10 miles southeast of the city on the way to The Strand, was Tongo's choice for experiencing the "real Africa." The name Gugulethu means "our pride" in Xhosa, the language spoken by 95 percent of the township's nearly 400,000 inhabitants. However, the pride associated with Gugulethu was questionable, as statistics from the South African Institute of Race Relations revealed that 730 people were murdered in the township between 2005 and 2010. This meant that, on average, someone was murdered there every 60 hours over the past five years.

Dewani continued his narrative. He explained that after their drive through the township, they had continued for another 22 miles to The Strand, where they had enjoyed a sushi dinner. Tongo had waited outside in his Sharan vehicle.

At 10:30 p.m., they had left the restaurant and decided to take another drive through Gugulethu on their way back to Cape Town. However, half an hour into the drive, they were ambushed by two armed men. The gunmen jumped onto the car's hood at a crossroad, forcing Tongo to stop. Tongo was then ordered to exit the car at gunpoint. One of the gunmen took control of the vehicle, with Dewani and Anni in the backseat. Anni was screaming as the car sped off. Twenty minutes later, at 11:20 p.m., the gunmen pushed

Dewani out through one of the car's rear windows, while the car continued into the dark night with Anni still inside.

Dewani recounted that he landed on a patch of sand after being thrown out of the moving car. He attempted to seek help by knocking on doors, but no one responded. Eventually, he managed to flag down a passing car and was driven back to the hotel, where he raised the alarm about the incident. The following day, he spoke to The Daily Mail, a London newspaper, and shared his ordeal over the phone.

Sympathy and suspicion

Dewani's father, Prakash, and Anni's father, Vinod Hindocha, boarded a flight from London to Cape Town, attracting global media attention to their love story. Anni Hindocha, born to Indo-Ugandan parents in Sweden, grew up in

Mariestad and later moved to England, where she met Shrien Dewani. Dewani, the son of millionaire Prakash, was a successful businessman himself, involved in the healthcare industry. After their engagement in June 2010, they had a lavish wedding in Mumbai, India.

Following their wedding, the couple celebrated the Hindu festival of Diwali with the Dewani family in Bristol before embarking on their honeymoon in South Africa. They stayed at a game reserve near the Kruger National Park, enjoying the wildlife and relaxation. On their way to Cape Town, instead of using the airport shuttle, they took a taxi driven by Zola Tongo, arranged by Dewani's office in Bristol.

The incident raised questions about their decision to drive through townships, known for their high crime rates. The English media highlighted the dangers of South Africa, while the South African media questioned Dewani's version of events. The South African police commissioner and the country's minister of Tourism and Economic Development defended South Africa's reputation and provided support to Dewani.

Both the Dewani and Hindocha families stood by Shrien during this difficult time, with condolences pouring in from Bristol and Sweden. The incident sparked discussions about the impact on tourism in Cape Town, a popular destination for millions of foreign visitors each year.After Anni's body underwent an autopsy, Shrien Dewani hired Billy Gundelfinger, a prominent divorce and criminal lawyer based in

Johannesburg, to represent him. However, Gundelfinger resigned shortly afterward, citing client confidentiality as the reason for his departure.

The South African police, known for their secrecy, disclosed limited information about the autopsy. They confirmed that Anni had not been sexually assaulted. Regarding her murder, they revealed that her body was discovered in the carjacked Sharan vehicle in Gugulethu's Lingelethu West area. Gugulethu is a township with a population of 40,000. The carjackers and murderers had forced Dewani out of the car in the neighboring township of Khayelitsha, which is home to over 400,000 people, primarily young individuals. Khayelitsha is one of the country's most impoverished townships, although its crime rate has been decreasing in recent years. The police attributed this reduction to the cooperation of residents in combating crime, such as reporting criminals.

On November 16, Dewani and the two fathers flew back to England, accompanied by Anni's body, which was transported in the cargo hold of a plane. Many people in South Africa questioned why the police had allowed Dewani to leave the country, as they believed he should have stayed in Cape Town to assist with the investigation and identify the killers. However, Commissioner Cele explained that Dewani was not considered a suspect, so they could not detain him against his will.

Investigation

As the media continued to speculate about the murder, the South African police maintained their vague approach. In response to criticism about their lack of cooperation, Minister of Community Safety Albert Fritz stated that the search for Mrs. Dewani's killers was at a crucial stage, and they did not want to risk jeopardizing the investigation by revealing details.

Police Minister Nathi Mthethwa and Commissioner Cele urged residents of the three townships to come forward with any information that could help apprehend the killers, whom Mthethwa referred to as "scoundrels." At the same time, Minister Mthethwa emphasized the role of foreign tourists in ensuring their own safety while vacationing in the country. He advised them to exercise caution and seek information from reliable tourist resources instead of asking strangers for directions.

On November 16, Captain Frederick van Wyk of the Cape Town police announced that his team was working on leads, but provided no further details. The following day, a 26-year-old man named Xolile Mngeni was arrested in Lingelethu township. He was taken into custody along with his younger brother from their grandmother's house. Mngeni denied any involvement in Anni's murder, although the police discovered a gun, empty bullet cartridges, and Anni's stolen belongings (wristwatch, white-gold and diamond bracelet, handbag, and cell phone) at his grandmother's house. Mngeni's lawyer claimed that the police had subjected him to suffocation using a plastic bag during interrogation.

Two days later, two more individuals were arrested: Mziwamadoda Qwabe, 25, from

Lingelethu, and Zola Tongo, 31, the taxi driver. Tongo, who resided in Bothasig, a middle-income town near Cape Town, was not a regular employee of the limousine hire company that owned the Sharan vehicle; he was working on the side. Qwabe's lawyer also alleged mistreatment by the police during his client's arrest and questioning, claiming that they had kicked and beaten him.

Initially, Tongo insisted that he was a victim like the Dewanis, but he eventually changed his story and confessed. He informed the police that Dewani had paid him $2,500 to arrange Anni's murder. This revelation made headlines worldwide due to the tragic nature of a beautiful woman being cold-bloodedly killed on her honeymoon. Dewani vehemently denied any involvement in a contract killing or being the one who orchestrated it. To help convey his message, he enlisted the services of Max Clifford, a well-known English PR guru.

Anni Dewani's body was cremated in Bristol according to Hindu customs, and a memorial service was held for her in her birthplace of Mariestad, Sweden.

Tongo's tale

According to Tongo's account, he first encountered the Dewani couple on Friday, November 12, when he picked them up from the Cape Town airport to drive them to their hotel. During the ride, the couple asked him if he could take them on sightseeing tours and offered to pay him in cash for each excursion.

About half an hour after dropping off the Dewanis at the Cape Grace Hotel, Tongo was waiting outside in case they wanted to go on another drive when Dewani approached him. Tongo claims that Dewani asked if he knew someone who could "eliminate" a person for him.

The following day, Saturday, November 13, while driving Dewani to a black-market money dealer to exchange some US dollars for South African rand, they discussed the murder plan. Tongo then drove Dewani back to the hotel within an hour.

The target of the planned murder was Anni Dewani, who was to be killed in a staged carjacking. Dewani informed Tongo that he had already arranged a similar fake carjacking murder in South Africa in the past. However, Tongo admitted that he didn't have the expertise to carry out the killing himself or know anyone who did. He did, however, know someone named Monde Mbolombo, a 31-year-old hotel receptionist at the Hotel Colosseum near Cape Town, who had connections in the criminal underworld and could help find a hitman.

Tongo approached Mbolombo and informed him that there would be a payment of R15,000 ($2,500) for the job. Mbolombo requested R5,000 ($1,000) for finding a hitman and stated that the hitman would need to be paid R10,000

($1,500). It is unclear if the total amount offered by Dewani was $5,000 as the police have not confirmed this.

Mbolombo knew two potential killers who could carry out the murder: Mngeni and Qwabe.

On the evening of the planned murder, Tongo picked up the couple from the hotel in his Sharan vehicle, and the staged carjacking scheme that Tongo and Dewani had devised together was set in motion. Tongo drove the couple to the predetermined location in Gugulethu township where the two killers were supposed to be waiting. However, they were nowhere to be seen. Tongo proceeded to drive to The Strand for the dinner that Anni believed was the purpose of their outing. Before reaching the restaurant, Tongo sent a text message to Dewani's

Blackberry, reminding him about the money. Dewani responded from the rear seat, informing Tongo that the money was in an envelope behind the front passenger seat. Outside the restaurant, Dewani approached Tongo and inquired about the situation, instructing him to ensure that the job was done that night. While the couple dined, Tongo called the killers to inquire about their whereabouts earlier and to confirm that they would be at the agreed-upon location in Gugulethu from 11 o'clock onwards..

They put a gun in my ear

In Bristol, Dewani, visibly distressed with red and sunken eyes, defended himself and recounted the carjacking incident. Speaking to the Daily Mail, he stated, "I don't want to go into detail about what happened during the attack because I will probably start crying. But they were so cold. They put a gun to my ear and pulled the trigger. It felt like something from a movie. The two men kept assuring us, 'We won't hurt you. We just want the car.' That was a lie. Most of the conversation in the car consisted of us begging to be released together. I held onto Anni and pleaded with them, 'If you're not going to harm her, why don't you let us go?'"

However, Dewani's account had undergone some changes. He claimed that it was Tongo who suggested driving through Gugulethu township, and they only entered the township once, after dining in The Strand. He also mentioned that he and his wife were held captive in the car for 40 minutes before he was thrown out, contradicting his previous statement of 20 minutes. Dewani admitted to struggling with the two assailants, but they overpowered him and forcibly ejected him from the vehicle. They took his Blackberry, but upon returning to the hotel, he desperately tried, without success, to contact Anni's cell phone company to trace her phone. He also made strenuous but unsuccessful attempts to obtain the Sharan's registration number. When his efforts proved fruitless, he pleaded with the police to deploy a helicopter to search for the car over Cape Town.

Describing his late wife, Dewani said she cherished life and had always been a joyful person. In response to Tongo's version of events on the night of the murder, he questioned, "I searched high and low for my perfect partner... why would I want to kill her?" Dewani claimed that he and Anni had taken a romantic walk along the beach before returning to the Sharan. The restaurant they visited was located by the seaside, and he fondly recalled holding hands with his wife.

PR guru Clifford, as well as both the Dewani and Hindocha families, vehemently rejected Tongo's account of the murder night, considering it outrageous. However, Ashok Hindocha, Anni's uncle, stated that the South African police should further investigate the murder. He also expressed the belief that Shrien Dewani should return to South Africa to clear his name. Hindocha emphasized that the entire Hindocha family was eager to discover who was responsible for their daughter's murder and the motive behind it. He added, "If it was my wife who was murdered, I would jump on a plane, go there, and ask those people, 'Why did you kill my wife and for what?' This is a question not only the Hindocha family, but millions of people around the world, would like to have answered."

Talk

While the South African media openly favored Tongo's account over Dewani's, individuals who knew the widower and had been acquainted with Anni began to share their perspectives. Preyen Dewani, Sheen's brother, described him as remarkably resilient and possessing strong character, firmly rooted in his Hindu faith. A former teacher of Dewani characterized him as an exceptional young man, highly talented, diplomatic, and a natural leader.

Angela Bartlett, a 46-year-old woman from England, provided photographs to the London tabloid The Sun that she had taken during a vacation at the Chitwa Chitwa lodge in the Sabi Sand Game Reserve. The Dewanis were also guests at the lodge, and Bartlett had captured images of them dining with her and her husband on the first night of their honeymoon, four days before Anni's tragic death. Bartlett remarked, "They appeared to be a normal, happy couple. We never witnessed any arguments. They seemed to be well-matched, with Anni not overshadowed by Shrien. I was struck by Anni's beauty; she was stunning."

Dinho Plembe, a bartender at the lodge, didn't perceive the couple as deeply in love. He shared with the South African media, "I never saw them kiss, cuddle, or hold hands. If I hadn't been told they were on their honeymoon, I wouldn't have guessed it."

Anni's father, Vinod Hindocha, voiced concerns similar to those of his brother Ashok regarding the South African police's handling of the case. He questioned why his son-in-law was allowed to leave the country merely four days after his daughter's murder and why a second autopsy on Anni's body had not been conducted, as rumors had circulated suggesting she had been sexually assaulted. The English authorities had also not conducted an autopsy. While expressing the desire for hisWhile the South African media openly favored Tongo's account over Dewani's, individuals who knew the widower and had been acquainted with Anni began to share their perspectives. Preyen Dewani, Sheen's brother, described him as remarkably resilient and possessing strong character, firmly rooted in his Hindu faith. A former teacher of Dewani characterized him as an exceptional young man, highly talented, diplomatic, and a natural leader.

Angela Bartlett, a 46-year-old woman from England, provided photographs to the London tabloid The Sun that she had taken during a vacation at the Chitwa Chitwa lodge in the Sabi Sand Game Reserve. The Dewanis were also guests at the lodge, and Bartlett had captured images of them dining with her and her husband on the first night of their honeymoon, four days before Anni's tragic death. Bartlett remarked, "They appeared to be a normal, happy couple.

We never witnessed any arguments. They seemed to be well-matched, with Anni not overshadowed by Shrien. I was struck by Anni's beauty; she was stunning."

Dinho Plembe, a bartender at the lodge, didn't perceive the couple as deeply in love. He shared with the South African media, "I never saw them kiss, cuddle, or hold hands. If I hadn't been told they were on their honeymoon, I wouldn't have guessed it."

Anni's father, Vinod Hindocha, voiced concerns similar to those of his brother Ashok regarding the South African police's handling of the case. He questioned why his son-in-law was allowed to leave the country merely four days after his daughter's murder and why a second autopsy on Anni's body had not been conducted, as rumors had circulated suggesting she had been sexually assaulted. The English authorities had also not conducted an autopsy. While expressing the desire for his son-in-law to return to South Africa to officially identify the two killers and the taxi driver, Vinod Hindocha called the London-based Sunday tabloid The Mail on Sunday from his home in Sweden to share that Anni had burst into tears during the flight from London to South Africa and had refused to sit next to her husband.

When asked how he had learned about this, Mr. Hindocha declined to provide further details. However, he did release a statement stating, "Further to recent reports in several newspapers,

I would like to state that my relationship with Shrien is a good one, and I love him like a son. Whoever did this to my daughter are criminals who need to be caught and put behind bars. I have always supported Shrien, and I will continue to do so throughout this horrendous ordeal."

By this point, the South African police had begun to insist that Dewani must return to Cape Town to assist with their investigation. They made it clear that if he did not return voluntarily, South Africa would seek his extradition from England. However, Dewani, refusing to return, hired Clare Montgomery QC, a London-based lawyer specializing in criminal and fraud law. In response to English journalists, Dewani stated, "Claiming that I was somehow involved simply defies logic. Anni wasn't listed on any life insurance policies, and we hadn't even made a will. I had no motive, whether financial or otherwise. I loved her, and I still do."

Tongo's trial

On Monday, December 6, the trial of Zola Tongo began in Cape Town's High Court, just 24 days after Anni's murder. Despite it being summer in South Africa, a sense of gloom hung over the city's Dutch-style houses, with a white cloud hovering above Table Mountain, a reminder of the country's Dutch history. Tongo arrived at the courthouse in a police transport vehicle, attempting to conceal his face within his white shirt.

In front of a crowded courtroom, State Prosecutor Rodney de Kock presented a clear case implicating Shrien Dewani. Tongo confirmed the story he had previously told the police, which had received extensive media coverage. He stated that he and Dewani had agreed that they would be unharmed, while Anni, the female occupant of the car, would be killed. Tongo had received ZAR5,000 ($700) as his share of the money Dewani had offered for the murder.

Judge President John Hlophe remarked, "The alleged carjacking was, in fact, not a carjacking, but part of a plan devised by Shrien Dewani, the husband of the deceased, and the accused to conceal the true facts, namely that the deceased was murdered at the request of her husband."

Finally, Prosecutor de Kock explained the terms of a plea bargain that had been agreed upon with Tongo. Before the abolition of the death penalty in South Africa in 1997, the punishment for murder, including complicity in murder, was execution by hanging. However, in present-day South Africa, the maximum sentence for murder is life imprisonment, which entails a minimum of 28 years in prison before parole can be considered. Due to the plea bargain, Tongo received a reduced sentence of 18 years for his complicity in the murder.

Tongo still shielded his face as he was led out of the courtroom and the courthouse.

Mngeni and Qwabe were scheduled to stand trial in February 2011. As for Mbolombo, he was granted immunity from prosecution on the condition that he continued to cooperate with the police and provide truthful testimony in the trials of Mngeni and Qwabe, as well as in the potential trial of Shrien Dewani in South Africa. Mbolombo had confessed to the police that the day after Anni's murder, he had asked Qwabe about the events of the previous night. Qwabe's response had been, "Haven't you heard the news? It was all over the news."

Truths or untruths?

Despite Tongo's conviction and the imprisonment of Mngeni and Qwabe, the Dewani name continued to make headlines. Some newspapers in London claimed to have access to closed-circuit television footage showing Anni walking through the lobby of Chitwa Chitwa Lodge with her head down, focusing on a laptop. According to these reports, the South African police believed that the laptop could contain valuable information about the couple's relationship, such as whether they had arguments or realized their marriage was a mistake. However, the laptop was missing.

The editors of these papers also mentioned another footage from Cape Grace Hotel's security cameras, showing Dewani handing Tongo a bag that the latter concealed under his clothes before entering a restroom. It was speculated that Tongo went to the restroom to count the money, possibly dividing it into four parts to pay his three accomplices. This scene was recorded two days after Anni's murder, supporting Tongo's claim that Dewani had paid him on that day.

Additionally, several leaks about the case were reported. One verified leak was about Dewani misleading Chitwa Chitwa Lodge to obtain a discount by claiming to be a high-ranking English tourism official during the couple's reservation process.

However, there were unverified leaks, including Dewani's alleged attempt to get a refund for the unused portion of Anni's air ticket from London to Cape Town, the claim that the Dewanis' care home business was in $10.3 million debt, and the assertion that Shrien and Anni's marriage was arranged by their families rather than a love match.

Another significant leak involved Dewani mentioning a person named Dr. Pox Raghavjee, who had been killed in a carjacking in King William's Town, a town located around 600 miles from Cape Town. The doctor was a friend of the Dewanis, and this leak raised suspicions.

The most damaging leak to Dewani's reputation and his claim of innocence in his wife's murder was the connection to Dr. Raghavjee's murder. The South African police had ruled out robbery as a motive for the doctor's killing, as his wallet with cash, gold watch, and cell phone were not taken. This leak cast doubt on Dewani's character and raised questions about his involvement in both cases.

South Africa's legal counsel in England, Ben Watson, requested the English police to arrest Shrien Dewani and hold him until an extradition hearing could be conducted. The Cape Town police wanted to question Dewani not only about his wife's murder but also about Dr. Raghavjee's murder.

On Tuesday, December 7, Dewani, dressed in blue jeans and a dark-blue windbreaker, surrendered to the English police in Bristol. Commissioner Cele in South Africa referred to him as a "monkey," which only served to exacerbate old colonial wounds and prejudices.

The following day, Dewani appeared before the City of Westminster Magistrates' Court in London and was initially granted bail. However, before leaving the courtroom, Watson successfully had the judge's permission for bail revoked. Consequently, Dewani, looking devastated and in deep shock, was taken to London's Wandsworth Prison, where he would remain until a decision regarding extradition was reached. His fellow inmate in the prison was Julian Assange of WikiLeaks, who was also awaiting an extradition decision.

A day later, bail was eventually granted to Dewani. The Dewani family paid a bail surety of $388,000 and Dewani, wearing an electronic tag, was allowed to return to Bristol. He was subjected to a home curfew, with permission to leave his residence only once a day to report to the local police.

Public relations expert Max Clifford expressed the family's satisfaction with the bail decision, stating that Dewani would continue to receive bereavement and trauma counseling.

Through his lawyer, Dewani made it clear that he intended to fight against extradition to South Africa and had no intention of returning voluntarily.

What now?

Ami Denborg, Anni's sister, stated from her residence in Sweden that if Dewani were guilty, his actions would be unforgivable. However, she declined to engage in a discussion about whether

her family believed he was guilty. The Hindocha and Dewani families had severed contact, with their last communication occurring before Tongo accused Shrien Dewani in the Cape Town court of orchestrating Anni's murder.

Speaking to The Mirror on New Year's Day from his home in Sweden, Vinod Hindocha expressed the sadness of ending the year without Anni but refrained from accusing his son-in-law of his daughter's murder. He questioned why Dewani, if innocent, would be afraid and suggested that if he truly loved Anni, he should return to South Africa and help identify her killers.

The extradition hearing was expected to take place in London in the coming weeks, and the

South African police believed they had a strong case against Dewani. Max Clifford, his PR representative, described Dewani as being in a terrible state and regretting ever going to South Africa for his honeymoon. Clifford maintained that Dewani had fully cooperated with the South African authorities and answered all their questions.

In December, after allegations emerged regarding Dewani's potential connection to Dr. Raghavjee's murder, Clifford dismissed the claims as flimsy and ridiculous, stating that it would be a farce or comedy if it weren't for the tragedy involved. However, the situation remained serious, and nobody found it amusing. Neither the Hindocha family, nor the Dewani family, and certainly not Shrien Dewani, who turned 31 on December 29, were in a laughing mood. Dewani faced the daunting task of clearing his name.

The legal proceedings seemed like a complicated maze with numerous twists and turns. The first Christmas and New Year's after Anni's murder had passed. Dewani remained confined to his luxurious Bristol residence, and his electronic tag did not trigger any alarms.

At the end of January, in scorching Cape Town, a preliminary hearing took place at the Wynberg court. The two accused, Mngeni and Qwabe, did not attend the hearing but were represented by their respective lawyers. Captain Hendrikse, the senior investigating officer, read an affidavit in court where Qwabe admitted that while driving the hijacked car after Shrien was thrown out, he heard a single gunshot from the rear seat where Mngeni sat next to Anni. Qwabe became nervous, pulled the car over, and saw Mngeni searching for the bullet shell on all fours. Qwabe joined him, found the shell, and threw it into a nearby drain before fleeing.

Captain Hendrikse did not mention in court that Qwabe had previously denied in his police testimony any plot by Shrien Dewani to have his wife killed. The omission was noted by The Daily Mail, a London-based publication that seemed to support Shrien Dewani. The article questioned why, if they had planned to kill Anni, they would have done it in a location where they could properly dispose of the weapon and hide the body.

In mid-February, Shrien made headlines once again as he was rushed to the hospital after collapsing at home. Reports suggested that he had attempted suicide, but his family immediately denied this claim, stating that he was suffering from post-traumatic stress, according to Max Clifford. However, subsequent media reports indicated that he had ingested 46 prescription pills with the intention of ending his life. Nonetheless, his extradition hearing, scheduled for May 3, would proceed.During a preliminary extradition hearing on Monday, March 21, the London court ordered Shrien Dewani to check into a psychiatric clinic based on a psychiatric report about his mental state. He chose to stay at The Priory, a renowned five-star psychiatric clinic in Bristol where celebrities like Kate Moss, Robbie Williams, and Ronnie Wood have sought treatment in the past. Despite being in the clinic, he was still required to wear the electronic tag.

Meanwhile, in South Africa, the police announced to the media that their investigation into Anni's murder was mostly complete and expressed confidence in extraditing Shrien to Cape Town to stand trial for orchestrating his wife's murder.

However, Shrien's stay at The Priory was short-lived. On Monday, April 11, he was moved, reportedly with his consent, to a secure mental hospital called The Cygnet Hospital Kewstoke, which overlooks the Bristol Channel. The media received a vague explanation from PR representative Clifford, stating that Shrien had not been very happy and that there had been some dramas. Subsequent reports in the following days shed light on the truth.

According to an unidentified mental health worker, Shrien had become loud and disruptive, allegedly throwing a plate at another patient during an argument and throwing a cushion at a nurse. The health worker shared that other patients were frightened and intimidated by Shrien. Additionally, Shrien left the clinic in a rage, breaking one of his bail conditions.

His time at The Cygnet Hospital was also brief. Within two weeks, a court in London sectioned him under the Mental Health Act and transferred him to the secure unit of Blackberry Hill Hospital near Bristol. The Cygnet Hospital was unable to handle his increasingly erratic and aggressive behavior.

On Tuesday, May 3, the extradition hearing took place at London's Belmarsh Magistrate's Court as scheduled, but Shrien was absent. The hearing was adjourned until a later date, potentially in July, or until a psychiatric evaluation declared him mentally fit.

In South Africa, the media prepared for the trial of Mngeni and Qwabe, scheduled for

Wednesday, June 1. Cape Town experienced an early arrival of winter, with a cold breeze and drizzle affecting the photographers waiting outside the Wynberg courthouse.Only Qwabe arrived at the courthouse in Cape Town, coming from Pollsmoor Prison, while Mngeni's whereabouts were unknown. A search was conducted, and it was later revealed that Mngeni had fallen ill and had been transferred to the prison's hospital with a severe headache and disorientation. The trial was adjourned to a later date, and it was uncertain whether Mngeni would be able to stand trial due to his illness. Legal experts doubted that Shrien would be extradited to South Africa, considering the mishandling of Mngeni's situation by the police. Anni's family and friends expressed frustration with Shrien for allegedly hiding the truth about what happened that night in Cape Town. An anonymous friend of Anni revealed that she had sent messages expressing emotional distress before the murder, and it was also mentioned that Anni had thrown her engagement ring at Shrien and expressed dissatisfaction with their relationship. The police claimed to have evidence that Shrien orchestrated Anni's murder, but some individuals, like a mosque member who knew Shrien, believed in his innocence. Anni's ashes were scattered in Sweden, and the Hindocha family made it clear that the Dewanis were not welcome at the ceremony. The trial was postponed due to Mngeni's surgery, and it was expected that Shrien would be extradited by August 2 and held in a Cape Town jail.Only Qwabe arrived at the courthouse in Cape Town, coming from Pollsmoor Prison, while Mngeni's whereabouts were unknown. A search was conducted, and it was later revealed that Mngeni had fallen ill and had been transferred to the prison's hospital with a severe headache and disorientation. The trial was adjourned to a later date, and it was uncertain whether Mngeni would be able to stand trial due to his illness. Legal experts doubted that Shrien would be extradited to South Africa, considering the mishandling of Mngeni's situation by the police. Anni's family and friends expressed frustration with Shrien for allegedly hiding the truth about what happened that night in Cape Town. An anonymous friend of Anni revealed that she had sent messages expressing emotional distress before the murder, and it was also mentioned that Anni had thrown her engagement ring at Shrien and expressed dissatisfaction with their relationship. The police claimed to have evidence that Shrien orchestrated Anni's murder, but some individuals, like a mosque member who knew Shrien, believed in his innocence. Anni's ashes were scattered in Sweden, and the Hindocha family made it clear that the Dewanis were not welcome at the ceremony. The trial was postponed due to Mngeni's surgery, and it was expected that Shrien would be extradited by August 2 and held in a Cape Town jail.

But no: No trial yet

On Tuesday, August 2, significant developments occurred in the case. Both Shrien Dewani and Xolile Mngeni were absent from the court proceedings. Earlier, on July 19, Shrien's extradition hearing in London had been postponed due to concerns about his mental state, with his lawyers claiming that he was suicidal. He was sent back to Blackberry Hill Hospital near Bristol for further evaluation. Xolile Mngeni, on the other hand, was suffering from a brain tumor called pineoblastoma, which was deteriorating his health. Medical reports revealed that even if the cancer was treated, he would not be able to stand trial due to his medical condition.

Only Qwabe, one of the accused, was present in the courtroom. His lawyer expressed frustration at the prolonged delay of the trial, which was taking a toll on Qwabe's mental well-being. The trial for both Qwabe and Mngeni was rescheduled for Tuesday, September 20, although there were doubts about Mngeni's ability to face justice at that time.

Despite the setbacks, Anni Dewani's family and friends, as well as the global community following the case, remained hopeful that Shrien's next extradition hearing on August 10 would result in his extradition to South Africa. On that date, the judge ruled in favor of extradition, dismissing arguments regarding Shrien's mental health and potential risks in South African prisons. However, it was noted that the judge's decision was not final, as it would be up to Home Secretary Theresa May to make the ultimate decision after reviewing the extensive Dewani dossier.

The possibility of an appeal in the High Court and the requirement for the South African police to establish Shrien's involvement in organizing Anni's murder before he could stand trial added further complexity to the case. In the meantime, rumors about Shrien's sexuality and doubts expressed by Anni regarding his virility continued to circulate. Leaked testimony from Shrien's previous fiance, Rani Kansagra,

confirmed the rumors and received significant media attention.

The case remained ongoing, with uncertainties surrounding Shrien's extradition and the legal proceedings that would follow. The focus shifted to the decisions of the Home Secretary and the future steps taken by Shrien's legal team.The media scrutiny intensified as the case dragged on, with various speculations and rumors circulating about Shrien Dewani and the circumstances surrounding Anni's murder. The public's interest remained high, and Anna's family and supporters continued to seek justice for her.

While awaiting the Home Secretary's decision, Shrien's legal team prepared for a potential appeal in the High Court to challenge the extradition ruling. They were determined to exhaust all legal avenues to prevent Shrien from being sent to South Africa to face trial.

In the midst of the legal proceedings, the emotional toll on both families was evident. Anni's loved ones grappled with the loss of their daughter and the painstaking wait for justice, while the Dewani family staunchly maintained Shrien's innocence and expressed their unwavering support for him.

As the weeks and months passed, the pressure mounted on Home Secretary Theresa May to review the case and make her final decision. The voluminous Dewani dossier had to be carefully examined, taking into account the legal arguments, medical assessments, and potential implications of extraditing Shrien to South Africa.

The media coverage continued to fuel public debate and speculation. The revelations about Shrien's previous engagement and the allegations surrounding his sexuality added further complexity to the narrative, casting a shadow over the already tragic circumstances.

Ultimately, the final outcome of the case remained uncertain. The Home Secretary's decision would determine whether Shrien Dewani would be extradited to South Africa to face questioning by the police and potentially stand trial. The legal battle and the pursuit of justice for Anni Dewani continued, leaving both families and the public eagerly awaiting the resolution of this high-profile and emotionally charged case.Beauty,

Wealth and Tragedy: The Death of Anni Dewani on Honeymoon

The names of the places evoked an exotic image: Gugulethu, Lingelethu, Khayelitsha, Chitwa Chitwa. They conjured visions of vibrant people dancing to the rhythmic beat of drums on a warm summer evening.

However, to the police officers clad in their somber dark blue uniforms, gathered around the abandoned white Volkswagen Sharan in Lingelethu, there was nothing exotic about the young woman sprawled across the back seat. The two bullet holes between her shoulders and another in her neck, which had caused her blood to spill, staining the car's interior, made it clear that she was dead.

The young woman was identified as Anni Dewani.

The officers grappled with the difficult task of informing her husband, Shrien, who had reported her missing earlier that morning and anxiously awaited news at a nearby luxury hotel.

It was Sunday, November 13, 2010, a little past 7 a.m. The day had already broken two hours prior, as is typical in Africa, where the sun rises early and darkness falls swiftly.

To be precise, this was South Africa, a country that had recently emerged from three centuries of institutionalized racial segregation, known as apartheid. However, South Africa was grappling with a high crime rate, which had become one of the highest among developing nations. Government statistics from September 2010 revealed a staggering number of serious crimes committed in the period from April 2009 to March 2010. Among them were 68,332 cases of rape, 17,410 attempted murders, 16,834 murders, 14,542 incidents of illegal firearm possession, 13,902 carjackings, 2,889 kidnappings, and 256,577 residential burglaries.

The police officers present at the scene were undoubtedly hardened individuals, yet even they found it difficult to process the magnitude of the situation.

Anni and Shrien Dewani were English tourists visiting South Africa.

They were enjoying their honeymoon.

After embarking on a safari in the northern part of the country, they had traveled south and checked into the luxurious five-star Cape Grace hotel in Cape Town, the parliamentary capital of South Africa.

The couple seemed to have everything to look forward to, but tragically, one of them was now dead: a victim of murder.

On the previous night, close to midnight, Shrien Dewani, a 30-year-old wealthy Anglo-Indian man from Bristol, England, had approached the hotel receptionist in distress. He reported that he and his 28-year-old wife, Anni, had been carjacked by two armed men while riding in a taxi. According to Dewani's account, the gunmen had driven off with Anni, leaving him behind.

The hotel staff immediately contacted the police, who hurried to the scene.

Given the circumstances, the police refrained from discussing luck with Dewani. They did not inform him that he was fortunate to have survived, as carjackings in South Africa often resulted in the death of the vehicle's occupants. They also chose not to disclose the grim reality that there was a high probability, around 99.99 percent, that the gunmen would have subjected Anni to sexual assault before potentially murdering her.

Dewani shared his version of events with the authorities.

He recounted that the previous evening, at around 8:30, they had hailed a taxi at the hotel with the intention of going to a restaurant in the upscale beach resort area of The Strand, located 31 miles southeast of Cape Town. In an effort to experience "the real Africa," as Dewani explained, they had requested the driver, a man named Zola Tongo, to take them through one of the nearby residential areas where Black African people lived. These areas, known as townships, had originated during the apartheid era when only white Europeans were allowed to reside in the cities and towns, while individuals of Black African, mixed-race, and Asian heritage were legally confined to the townships, also referred to as locations. Although constitutionalized apartheid had ended in 1994, a combination of housing shortages and poverty had prevented these ethnic groups from fully integrating into the previously exclusively white urban areas.

Life in the townships was characterized by insecurity and squalor, with residents living in shacks lacking electricity, hot water, and adequate heating during winter. However, these townships had become tourist attractions, as affluent foreigners believed they offered an opportunity to experience the "real Africa." Visitors could sample African cuisine cooked in traditional three-legged iron pots over open fires, savor frothy African beer, and dance to the vibrant rhythms of African music throughout the night.

Gugulethu, Lingelethu, and Khayelitsha were examples of such townships located in close proximity to Cape Town. Gugulethu, situated 10 miles southeast of the city on the route to The Strand, had been Tongo's choice to provide a taste of the "real Africa." The name Gugulethu means "our pride" in Xhosa, the language spoken by approximately 95 percent of the township's nearly 400,000 inhabitants. However, the pride associated with the township was debatable, considering that according to statistics from the South African Institute of Race Relations (SAIRR), 730 people had been murdered in Gugulethu between 2005 and 2010. This meant that, on average, a murder occurred in the township every 60 hours during that five-year period.

Dewani proceeded with his narrative.

According to Dewani's account, after their drive through the township, they continued for another 22 miles to The Strand, where they enjoyed a sushi dinner. Meanwhile, Tongo, the taxi driver, waited outside in his Sharan vehicle.

At around 10:30 p.m., they left the restaurant and began their journey back to Cape Town. Along the way, they decided to take another drive through Gugulethu. However, after approximately 30 minutes, their car was suddenly ambushed by two armed men. The gunmen jumped onto the car's hood at a crossroad, forcing Tongo to stop. Under the threat of their guns, Tongo was ordered out of the car, while one of the gunmen took control of the wheel. With Anni screaming in the back seat, the car sped away. Twenty minutes later, at 11:20 p.m., Dewani was pushed out of one of the car's rear windows while it was still in motion. He landed on a patch of sand.

Later, in a telephone interview with The Daily Mail, Dewani described the harrowing experience, saying, "I was dumped through the back of the passenger window as the car was moving. I landed on a patch of sand." Unable to find help despite knocking on doors, he eventually managed to flag down a passing car and was driven back to the hotel, where he raised the alarm.

As Shrien Dewani's father and Anni Hindocha's father boarded a flight from London to Cape Town, the love story between Shrien and Anni captured global attention, making headlines in South Africa, England, and beyond.

Anni Hindocha, born to Indo-Ugandan parents, grew up in Mariestad, Sweden, after her family sought asylum there in the 1970s due to anti-Asian violence in Uganda led by President Idi Amin. Anni excelled academically and became an electronic engineer, working for the Swedish electronic company Eriksson in Stockholm.

In 2009, she traveled to England and stayed with a cousin in Luton, north of London. It was there that she was introduced to Shrien Dewani, an equally attractive individual. Shrien, the son of millionaire Prakash Dewani and a millionaire himself, had a background as a former grammar school student and had been the general secretary of the National Hindu Students Forum at Manchester University. He had initially pursued a career in accounting but later joined his father and brother in establishing a chain of nursing and care homes for the elderly called PSP Healthcare, valued at $24 million.

After meeting Dewani, Anni moved to Bristol, situated 120 miles north, and began working at PSP. She also dabbled in fashion modeling. In June 2010, Anni and Dewani got engaged, and on October 28, they tied the knot in a grand three-day ceremony in Mumbai, India. The wedding, costing $310,000, was attended by 300 guests who had traveled from England and Sweden. The festivities included a dance by the radiant couple to the popular Bollywood song "Pehla Nasha" (First Love). Those in attendance remarked on the obvious love between the two. Anni wore a green sarong, while Dewani donned a traditional gold-colored Indian wedding suit with a turban.

Following the wedding, the couple returned to Bristol on November 3 to celebrate the Hindu festival of Diwali with the Dewani family in their luxurious residence located in the affluent Bristol suburb of Westbury-on-Trym.On November 7, just 10 days into their marriage, Shrien and Anni embarked on their honeymoon by flying from Cape Town to Johannesburg. From there, they took another flight north to Nelspruit and then had a 45-minute car journey to reach the Sabi Sand game reserve, which is adjacent to the Kruger National Park. They had made reservations at the Chitwa Chitwa Lodge, where they could relax by the swimming pool or participate in photo safaris. Hunting was strictly prohibited in both the Kruger National Park and the Sabi Sand Game Reserve.

After four days, on November 12, they traveled back to Nelspruit to catch a flight to Johannesburg and then proceed south to Cape Town. Instead of using the airport's shuttle service to their hotel, they opted for a Volkswagen Sharan taxi driven by Zola Tongo. Dewani's office in Bristol had arranged for the taxi in advance. It is common knowledge among tourists that driving through townships is dangerous due to the prevalence of carjackings. However, Dewani and Anni ventured into the townships not once, but twice, on the same night, prompting questions and doubts from both the South African police and the public regarding their decision-making. Many began questioning the credibility of Dewani's account, while the British media amplified stories depicting South Africa as a dangerous destination. This fueled old colonial biases and doubts about the country's ability to govern itself, with previous concerns raised about its suitability as the host of the 2010 Football World Cup. South Africa's high crime rate was emphasized as a contributing factor.

The English media used the Dewani murder as evidence to support the notion that South Africa was not the peaceful "rainbow nation" that Nelson Mandela had envisioned. The South African media, in response to these criticisms, raised significant questions. Why wasn't Dewani killed as well? If he was forcibly thrown out of a moving car, why did he not sustain any injuries? Why was the taxi driver spared? It was assumed that the two assailants would have understood that both Dewani and Tongo could potentially identify them to the police. Most importantly, the media questioned the sanity of a man who agreed to be driven through a township in the middle of the night, especially with his wife in the vehicle.

Bheki Cele, the commissioner of the South African police, responded angrily to English journalists who had come to Cape Town to cover the story, stating that the United Kingdom is not without crime.

Alan Winde, South Africa's Minister of Tourism and Economic Development, defended his country by highlighting the assistance provided to Shrien Dewani, stating that a team was available 24/7 to offer emotional, medical, and logistical support.

Cape Town receives 1.5 million foreign tourists annually, making it one of the world's fastest-growing tourist destinations. Local newspapers emphasized that if tourists were to stop visiting the city, the livelihoods of millions of people from all ethnic groups in the country would be affected.

Both the Dewani and Hindocha families supported Shrien in his grief, with the fathers flying to South Africa and condolences being offered at their respective homes in Bristol and Sweden.

During the autopsy conducted on Anni's body, Shrien hired Billy Gundelfinger, a Johannesburg-based lawyer specializing in divorce and criminal cases, to represent him.

However, Gundelfinger resigned on December 4, citing client confidentiality as the reason.

The South African police provided limited information, stating that Anni had not been raped in the autopsy report. They confirmed that her body was found in the carjacked Volkswagen Sharan in the Gugulethu sector named Lingelethu West, a township with a population of 40,000. Dewani had been forced out of the car earlier in the nearby township of Khayelitsha, home to over 400,000 people and experiencing a decreasing crime rate in recent years.

On November 16, Dewani and the two fathers returned to England, while Anni's body was transported in the cargo hold of a plane. The decision to allow Dewani to leave the country puzzled many in South Africa, as they believed he should have remained in Cape Town to assist with the investigation and identify the killers. Commissioner Cele explained that Dewani was not a suspect and could not be held against his will.

The South African police maintained their vague approach to the investigation, citing the need to avoid jeopardizing the process by revealing details. Minister Albert Fritz of Community Safety defended the police's non-cooperation in response to criticism.Police Minister Nathi Mthethwa and Commissioner Cele urged residents of the three townships to provide information that could lead to the apprehension of the killers, whom Mthethwa referred to as "scoundrels."

Minister Mthethwa also emphasized the role of foreign tourists in ensuring their own safety while vacationing in the country. He advised them to exercise caution and utilize tourist information resources, such as obtaining maps from tourist offices instead of asking strangers for directions.

On November 16, Captain Frederick van Wyk of the Cape Town police announced that they were working on leads regarding the case. However, no further details were provided.

The following day, a 26-year-old man named Xolile Mngeni was arrested in the Lingelethu township. He was taken into custody along with his younger brother at their grandmother's house. Mngeni denied any involvement in Anni's murder, despite the police finding a gun, empty bullet cartridges, and stolen items belonging to Anni in his grandmother's house. Mngeni's lawyer claimed that the police had subjected him to mistreatment during interrogation, including partially suffocating him with a plastic bag.

Two days later, two more individuals were arrested. They were Mziwamadoda Qwabe, 25, from Lingelethu, and Zola Tongo, 31, the taxi driver. Tongo, who resided in the town of Bothasig, was not a regular employee of the limousine hire company that owned the Sharan; he was working as a moonlighting driver.

Qwabe, through his lawyer, also alleged mistreatment by the police upon his arrest and during questioning, claiming that he had been kicked and beaten.

As for Tongo, he would initially insist that he was as much a victim of Mngeni and Qwabe as the Dewanis. Quickly though he changed his story. He will talk, he told the police. Next, negotiating a plea bargain, he not only talked, he sang like a bird. Dewani, he said, had paid him $2,500 (ZAR15,000 - South African rand) to organize the killing of Anni.

While the revelation rolled off the presses of newspapers all over the world because it was such a sad story for such a beautiful woman to be so cold-bloodedly slain on her honeymoon, Dewani vehemently denied that his wife's murder was a contract killing and that he had been the contractor.

To assist him in putting his message across, he hired the English PR guru, Max Clifford.

Said Clifford, known rather for doing public relations for scantily-clad wannabees and politicians embroiled in sex or financial scandals, than for men enmeshed in murder: "I have met Dewani. I have spoken to him. I have looked him in the eye. I have talked it through. I have asked him all the questions that journalists have been asking and all circumstances and I totally believe him."

Anni Dewani was cremated in Bristol according to the Hindu religion, and a memorial service was held for her in her birthplace in Sweden, in Mariestad.

Tongo's tale

Tongo informed the police, "I told Mbolombo that there would be R15,000 ($2,500) for the job. Mbolombo said he wanted R5,000 ($1,000) for finding a hitman, and we would have to pay the hitman R10,000 ($1,500)." The police did not confirm whether the total amount offered by Dewani to the four individuals was $5,000.

Indeed, Mbolombo knew two individuals who could carry out the killing: Mngeni and Qwabe.

At 8:30 p.m. that evening, Tongo picked up the couple from the hotel in his Sharan, and the pre-planned fake carjacking was initiated in collaboration with Dewani.

He drove the couple to the designated spot in Gugulethu township where the two killers were supposed to be waiting. However, they were not present. Tongo continued driving to The Strand for the dinner that Anni believed was the purpose of their outing. Before reaching the restaurant, Tongo sent a text message to Dewani's Blackberry, reminding him about the money. Dewani responded from the back seat, informing Tongo that the money was in an envelope behind the front passenger seat. Outside the restaurant, Dewani approached Tongo and inquired about the situation, emphasizing that he wanted the job completed that night. While the couple dined, Tongo called the killers to inquire about their whereabouts earlier and to ensure they would be at the specified location in Gugulethu from 11 o'clock onwards.

In Bristol, Dewani, visibly distraught and grieving, defended himself.

He recounted the carjacking incident, stating, "But I don't want to provide detailed information about what happened during the attack because I might start crying. But they were so cold. They put a gun to my ear and pulled the trigger. It truly felt like something out of a movie. The two men kept saying, 'We are not going to hurt you. We just want the car.' That was a lie. Most of the conversation in the car involved us pleading to be released together. I held onto Anni and asked them, 'If you're not going to harm her, why don't you let us go?'"

However, his account had slightly changed.

He claimed that Tongo was the one who suggested driving through Gugulethu township. They had only entered the township once, after their dinner in The Strand. Additionally, he admitted that he and his wife were held in the car for 40 minutes before he was thrown out, contradicting his previous statement of 20 minutes. He had struggled with the two killers, but they overpowered him and forcibly ejected him from the vehicle. They had taken his Blackberry, and upon returning to the hotel, he desperately attempted to contact Anni's cell phone company to trace her phone using the hotel's phone but was unsuccessful. He also made strenuous but unsuccessful efforts to obtain the Sharan's registration number. Frustrated with the lack of assistance, he pleaded with the police to deploy a helicopter to search for the car in Cape Town.

Regarding his murdered wife, he described her as someone who cherished life and was always a joyful person.

In response to Tongo's account of the events on the night of the murder, he stated, "He claimed that Tongo was the one who suggested driving through Gugulethu township. They had only entered the township once, which was after their dinner in The Strand. He also admitted that he and his wife were held captive in the car for 40 minutes before he was thrown out, contrary to his previous statement of 20 minutes. Although he struggled with the two killers, they overpowered him and forcefully ejected him from the vehicle. They confiscated his Blackberry, and upon returning to the hotel, he frantically tried, but failed, to contact Anni's cell phone company using the hotel's phone to trace her phone. He also made arduous but unsuccessful attempts to obtain the Sharan's registration number. When no one could assist him, he implored the police to dispatch a helicopter to search for the car in Cape Town.

Regarding his deceased wife, he recalled that she adored life and was always a happy person.

In response to Tongo's version of the events on the night of the murder, he said, "I searched extensively for my ideal partner... why would I want to kill her?"

He further claimed that he and Tongo had taken a romantic stroll along the beach before getting back into the Sharan, as the restaurant was situated on the waterfront.

"It was a beautiful evening," he reminisced, noting that they had held hands.

PR guru Clifford rejected Tongo's account of the murder night, describing it as outrageous. The Dewani family and the Hindocha family shared the same sentiment.

Anni's uncle, Ashok Hindocha, aged 50, insisted that the South African police should delve deeper into the murder. However, he also stated that Shrien Dewani should return to South Africa to clear his name.

"All members of the Hindocha family want to know who and why our girl was murdered. I can tell you, if it were my wife who was murdered, I would jump on a plane, go there, and ask those people, 'Why did you kill my wife and for what?' This is a question that not only the Hindocha family but millions of people around the world would like to have answered."

While the South African media did not conceal the fact that they believed Tongo rather than Dewani, people who knew the widower and had known Anni began to talk about them.

Preyen Dewani described his brother as very resilient and a man with strength of character. "He has always been strong with a firm belief in his Hindu faith," he said.

A former teacher of Dewani described him as an outstanding young man, immensely talented, very diplomatic and a natural leader.

Angela Bartlett, 46, from England handed photographs to the London tabloid The Sun she had taken on a holiday she and her husband had spent at the Chitwa Chitwa lodge in the Sabi Sand Game Reserve. The Dewanis were fellow guests and Bartlett had photographed the two dining with her and her husband at the lodge on the first night of their honeymoon, and four days before Anni was to be shot dead.

"They seemed such a normal, happy couple. There were no arguments that we saw. They seemed very evenly matched. She wasn't in his shadow. I was struck by how beautiful Anni was. She was stunning," said Bartlett.

The impression the couple had made on Dinho Plembe, a barman at the lodge, was not of two people who were madly in love with each other.

He told the South African media: "I never saw them kissing each other or cuddling or holding hands. If I hadn't been told that they were on their honeymoon I wouldn't have guessed it."

Anni's father, Vinod Hindocha, echoed his brother Ashod's concern by questioning the South African police's handling of the case. He wondered why the police had allowed his son-in-law to leave the country just four days after his daughter's murder and why they had not conducted a second autopsy on his daughter's body; rumors had started to circulate that Anni had indeed been raped. The English also had not conducted an autopsy. (In another high-profile death on foreign soil – that of Princess Diana, the Princess of Wales – the English police had conducted their own autopsy following that of the French.

While expressing his desire for his son-in-law to return to South Africa to officially identify the two killers and the taxi driver, he called The Mail on Sunday, a London-based tabloid, from his residence in Sweden. He informed them that his daughter had burst into tears during the flight from London to South Africa and had refused to sit next to her husband.

According to him, "We have heard that the air hostess noticed they were sitting separately and Anni was crying. The air hostess apparently asked Anni if she would like to sit with Shrien, but Anni said no."

When asked how he learned about this, he declined to provide further details. However, he released a statement stating, "Further to recent reports in several newspapers, I would like to state that my relationship with Shrien is a good one, and I love him like a son. Whoever did this to my daughter are criminals who need to be caught and put behind bars. I have always supported Shrien, and I will continue to do so throughout this horrendous ordeal."

By that time, the South African police had started asserting that Dewani must return to Cape Town to assist with their investigation. They made it clear that if he did not return voluntarily, South Africa would seek his extradition from England.

Refusing to return, Shrien Dewani hired Clare Montgomery QC, a London-based lawyer specializing in criminal and fraud law. In response to English journalists, he stated, "Saying I was somehow involved simply defies logic. Anni wasn't on any life insurance policies, and we hadn't even made a will. I had no motive - financial or otherwise. I loved her and still love her."

Tongo's Trial:

On Monday, December 6, just 24 days after Anni's murder, Zola Tongo's trial began at Cape Town's High Court. Despite the summer season in South Africa, a white cloud hung over Table Mountain, serving as a reminder of the country's Dutch history.

Tongo arrived at the courthouse in a police transport vehicle, attempting to conceal his face with his white shirt. State Prosecutor Rodney de Kock presented a clear case implicating Shrien Dewani to a packed courtroom. Tongo confirmed the story he had previously told the police, which had received widespread media coverage. He stated that he and Dewani had agreed that they would be unharmed and ejected from the Sharan, while Anni, the female occupant, would be killed. Tongo received ZAR5,000 ($700) as his share of the money offered by Dewani for the killing.

Judge President John Hlophe stated that the alleged carjacking was not a carjacking at all, but rather a planned scheme by Shrien Dewani, the deceased's husband, and the accused to hide the true facts: that the deceased was murdered at the request of her husband.

Prosecutor de Kock then presented the details of a plea bargain agreement reached with Tongo. Prior to 1997, when South Africa abolished the death penalty, murder and complicity in murder were punishable by hanging. However, in present-day South Africa, the maximum sentence for murder is life imprisonment, which equates to 28 years in prison before parole can be considered. Tongo, who was found guilty of complicity in murder, received a reduced sentence of 18 years due to the plea bargain.

Tongo continued to shield his face as he was led out of the courtroom and the courthouse.

Mngeni and Qwabe were scheduled to go on trial in February 2011.

Mbolombo, on the other hand, was granted immunity from prosecution on the condition that he cooperated with the police and testified truthfully in the trials of Mngeni and Qwabe, as well as in the potential trial of Shrien Dewani in South Africa.

In his confession to the police, Mbolombo stated that the day after Anni's murder, he asked Qwabe about the events of the previous night. Qwabe's response was, "Did you not hear the news? It was all over the news."

Despite Tongo's sentencing and the imprisonment of Mngeni and Qwabe, with the likelihood of them remaining in prison for at least 28 years, the Dewani case continued to make headlines.

Some London newspapers claimed to have been shown CCTV footage depicting Anni walking through the lobby of the Chitwa Chitwa Lodge, with her head down and eyes focused on a laptop. According to the reports, South African police believed that the laptop could contain valuable information about the couple's relationship, such as whether they had arguments or realized that their marriage was a mistake. However, the laptop was missing.

The editors of these newspapers also mentioned another piece of CCTV footage sourced from the Cape Grace Hotel's security cameras. It allegedly showed Dewani handing a bag to Tongo, who concealed it under his clothes before entering a restroom. The police speculated that Tongo went to the restroom to count the money, possibly dividing it among his three accomplices. This scene was recorded two days after Anni's murder and aligned with Tongo's claim that Dewani had paid him on that day.

The papers also reported several leaks of information about the case.

Only one leak about how Dewani had tricked the Chitwa Chitwa Lodge into giving him a discount was verifiable. The lodge confirmed that when Dewani's office had made the couple's reservation, they had been told that Shrien Dewani was a high-ranking English tourism official and they had been asked for a generous discount.

Those leaks which could not be verified were:

- Dewani had tried to be refunded for that part of Anni's London/Cape Town return air ticket that she had not used.

- The Dewanis' care home business was $10.3 million in debt.

- Shrien and Anni's marriage had not been a love match; it had been arranged by their families.

- The person Dewani had spoken of when he had told Tongo that he had already had someone killed in South Africa was Dr. Pox Raghavjee. The doctor, a friend of the Dewanis, was shot to death in 2007 in a carjacking in a town named King William's Town, some 600 miles from Cape Town.

Dewani was a closet gay.

That last leak grew in substance when a London-based German taxi boy (male hooker) known on the gay scene in England as "The German Master," reported to the London police that Shrien Dewani had paid him for three kinky sex sessions between September 2009 and April 2010. The police did not name the German but some London tabloids ran photos of him in his working gear of black leather and military-style cap. As it is not a misdemeanor in England to pay a rent boy for sex unless there had been soliciting in a public place which had not happened in this case, there was no charge that the English police could bring against the German. The South African police did express the wish to have a word with him about Dewani's sexuality.

The leak that was the most damaging to Dewani's reputation and his claim of innocence in his wife's murder was the one about the murder of Dr. Raghavjee. The doctor's murder had remained unsolved but the South African police had ruled out robbery because the doctor's wallet which contained cash was not stolen and neither was his gold watch and cell phone.

Mrs. Raghavjee would come to Dewani's rescue by describing any link between her husband's murder and that of Anni as ridiculous because the two men had never even met, yet the South African police reopened the case.

South Africa's legal counsel in England, Ben Watson, requested the English police to arrest Shrien Dewani and to hold him until a hearing of extradition to South Africa could be held. The Cape Town police not only wanted to question him about his wife's murder but also about that of Dr. Raghavjee.

On the following day, Tuesday, December 7, Shrien Dewani turned himself in to the English police in Bristol, wearing blue jeans and a dark-blue windbreaker. In South Africa, Commissioner Cele referred to him as a derogatory term, exacerbating old colonial wounds and prejudices.

The day after, Dewani appeared before the City of Westminster Magistrates' Court in London. Initially granted bail, the judge later withdrew consent for bail at the request of Watson. Consequently, Dewani, visibly devastated and in a state of deep shock, was taken to Wandsworth

Prison in London, where he would remain until a decision regarding his extradition was reached. Julian Assange, the founder of WikiLeaks, was also held there, awaiting a decision on his own extradition.

A day later, bail was eventually granted to Dewani.

The Dewani family posted a bail surety payment of $388,000 and were able to take Dewani, who wore an electronic tag, back to Bristol. He was placed under a home curfew, with the allowance to leave only once a day to report to the local police.

Max Clifford, a public relations expert, expressed the family's satisfaction with the bail decision, stating that Dewani would continue to receive bereavement and trauma counseling.

Through his lawyer, Dewani made it clear that he intended to fight extradition to South Africa and had no plans to return voluntarily.

What comes next?

Anni's sister, Ami Denborg, aged 32, spoke from her home in Sweden, stating that if Dewani were guilty, his actions would be unforgivable. However, she declined to engage in a debate regarding her family's belief in his guilt. Communication between the Hindocha and Dewani families had ceased, with their last interaction occurring before Tongo accused Shrien Dewani of orchestrating Anni's murder in the Cape Town court.

On New Year's Day, Vinod Hindocha, speaking from his home in Sweden to The Mirror newspaper, expressed his sadness at ending the year without Anni and refrained from accusing his son-in-law of his daughter's murder.

He said, "If he didn't do it, what is he afraid of? If he truly loved her as he claims, he should return to South Africa and identify her killers."

The extradition hearing was expected to take place in London in the following weeks, and the South African police believed they had a strong case against Dewani.

"He is in an extremely distressed state. He deeply regrets ever going to South Africa for his honeymoon. He has fully cooperated with the

South African authorities and has answered all their questions," stated Max Clifford, the PR expert, when discussing his client, Shrien Dewani.

In December, after the allegation arose connecting Shrien Dewani to the murder of Dr. Raghavjee, Clifford expressed his opinion to the Daily Mail, saying, "How weak and absurd this whole situation is. If it wasn't so tragic, it would be a farce, a comedy."

However, no one found it amusing.

Not the Hindocha family, not the Dewani family, and certainly not Shrien Dewani, who turned 31 on December 29. He now faced the task of clearing his name.

A complex legal journey with countless twists and turns lay ahead.

The first Christmas after Anni Dewani's murder came and went, followed by the arrival of the New Year.

Shrien Dewani remained confined to his opulent home in Bristol, and his electronic tag never triggered an alert.

At the end of January, in scorching Cape Town, a preliminary hearing took place in the Wynberg suburb court. The two accused, Mngeni and Qwabe, did not attend the hearing but were represented by their respective lawyers.

During the court proceedings, Captain Hendrikse, the lead investigator in the case, read an affidavit on behalf of Qwabe. In the affidavit, Qwabe admitted that while he was driving the hijacked car after Shrien had been forced out, he heard a single shot coming from the rear seat, where Mngeni was seated next to Anni. Qwabe claimed that he became extremely nervous and pulled the car over to the side of the road. He then exited the vehicle and witnessed Mngeni searching for the bullet shell on all fours in the rear seat. Qwabe assisted him, found the shell, and threw it into a nearby drain before fleeing.

Captain Hendrikse did not mention in court that Qwabe had previously denied, in his testimony to the police, any involvement in a plot orchestrated by Shrien Dewani to murder his wife, Anni. The Daily Mail, based in London, pointed out this omission and stated, "When the gun suddenly went off, it came as a complete surprise to him (Qwabe). If they had planned to kill her, wouldn't they have done it somewhere they could dispose of the weapon properly? And for that matter, hide the body?" It was evident that the newspaper was taking Shrien Dewani's side.

Continuing to attract media attention, Shrien once again made headlines in mid-February when he collapsed at home and was rushed to the hospital. Reports suggested that he had attempted suicide, although his family immediately denied this claim. According to PR expert Max Clifford, Shrien was suffering from post-traumatic stress. However, subsequent media reports indicated that he had ingested 46 prescription pills with the intention of ending his life. Despite this incident, his extradition hearing, scheduled for May 3, would proceed as planned.

On Monday, March 21, during a preliminary extradition hearing in a London court, Shrien's mental state was assessed through a psychiatric report. As a result, the court ordered him to be admitted to a psychiatric clinic. He chose to stay at The Priory, a renowned five-star psychiatric facility in Bristol, where celebrities like Kate Moss, Robbie Williams, and Ronnie Wood have previously sought treatment. Despite his admission to the clinic, he still had to wear the electronic tag.

Meanwhile, in South Africa, the police informed the media that their investigation into Anni's murder was nearing completion, and they expressed confidence that Shrien would be extradited to Cape Town to face trial for allegedly orchestrating his wife's murder.

However, Shrien's time at The Priory was short-lived. On Monday, April 11, he was reportedly moved, seemingly with his consent, to a secure mental hospital called The Cygnet Hospital Kewstoke, which overlooks the Bristol Channel.

What exactly happened at The Priory? PR expert Clifford offered a vague explanation to the media, stating, "He hasn't been very happy. There have been some incidents."

However, the truth, as reported by the media in the following days, was quite different. Shrien's behavior had reportedly become disruptive and confrontational. According to an unidentified mental health worker, he had engaged in an argument with another patient and had thrown a plate at them. He had also thrown a cushion at a nurse. The Sun, a London tabloid, reported that other patients felt frightened and intimidated by him. Additionally, Shrien had allegedly stormed out of the clinic in a fit of rage, violating one of his bail conditions.

His stay at The Cygnet Hospital was also brief. Within two weeks, he was involuntarily transferred to the secure unit of Blackberry Hill Hospital near Bristol, as he had exhibited increasingly erratic and aggressive behavior that The Cygnet Hospital couldn't handle.

On Tuesday, May 3, the extradition hearing began at Belmarsh Magistrate's Court in London as scheduled, but Shrien was not present. The hearing was adjourned on the same day until a later date, possibly in July, or until a psychiatric evaluation could determine his mental state.

In South Africa, preparations were underway for the trial of Mngeni and Qwabe, scheduled to start on Wednesday, June 1. Winter arrived early in Cape Town, accompanied by a chilly breeze and a fine drizzle that troubled the photographers waiting outside the Wynberg courthouse.

Only Qwabe arrived at the courthouse from the maximum-security Pollsmoor Prison in Cape Town and was taken to the cells to await his summons to the courtroom.

The whereabouts of Mngeni remained unknown.

No one, including the police, guards, lawyers, and prosecutors, seemed to know where he was.

Amidst the courthouse's consternation over the apparent "loss" of an inmate by the country's police, a search was initiated throughout the building to locate Mngeni. However, he could not be found.

An hour later, with Qwabe still held in a cell downstairs, the prosecutors announced that they had located Mngeni after contacting Pollsmoor. He had fallen ill and had been transferred from his cell to the prison's hospital due to a severe headache and disorientation.

The trial was adjourned to Monday, June 13.

The South African and English media did not fail to unravel the facts of Mngeni's "sudden" illness.

It had not been sudden at all.

In the middle of March, Mngeni had begun to complain of headaches and started to behave like someone who had had too many drinks. Taken to the prison's hospital and from there to Cape Town's Groote Schuur Hospital where Professor Christiaan Barnard had performed the world's first heart transplant in 1967, he had undergone surgery to drain fluid from his brain. An MRI brain scan had then revealed that he had a malignant brain tumor. When he was supposed to be in court for the start of his trial, he was awaiting further surgery at Groote Schuur

Hospital to remove the tumor. Radiotherapy was awaiting him.

The Qwabe/Mngeni trial has been rescheduled for Monday, June 13, but few legal and medical experts in South Africa and England believe that Mngeni would be able to stand trial. Described as seriously ill he would more likely be lying close to death in the hospital.

The legal experts also believe that after the Mngeni muddle which points to incompetence on the part of the South African police, no British court would agree to extradite Shrien to South Africa to stand trial there. The British would not trust the evidence that the South Africans would provide of Shrien's guilt.

Anni's family and friends in England, Sweden and India, are however praising the South African police for how they had conducted their investigation, but they feel frustrated and angry at what they think is Shrien hiding the facts of what had happened that night in Cape Town. Some of them have openly voiced their thoughts to the media. Others have chosen to do so anonymously.

From what they said, the newly-wed Anni, it appears, had something troubling on her mind which she was going to discuss with her family on her return from the South African safari honeymoon.

One of those who wanted to remain anonymous was a girl friend of Anni's who lives in Mumbai, India, where Anni and Shrien were married.

She told the London tabloids that she and Anni exchanged SMS (text) messages on November 7 – six days before the murder. She asked Anni: "How r u? How are things?" and Anni replied: "I'm ok, crying has become my new hobby."

This friend also told the media that Anni had thrown her engagement ring at Shrien eight days before their Mumbai wedding. Anni had then told her that she was "glad it was over" and that she and Shrien were "just not compatible."

There was talk about Shrien's feelings too.

The German sadomasochist male hooker – he was identified by the English police as Munich-born Leopold Leisser, 39 years old – said in the extradition hearing of May 3, that

Shrien had told him that he wanted to "find a way out" of marrying Anni.

He said that in April 2010, in other words seven months before the lavish Mumbai wedding ceremony, Dewani, a client, told him that although Anni was "a nice, lovely girl who he liked" he did not want to marry her but that he could not "break out of the engagement" because he would be disowned by his family. "He went on to say he needed to find a way out of it," said the hooker. The "it" was the marriage to Anni. Shrien had already "broken out" of an engagement. Before he had met Anni he had become betrothed to the daughter of the Indian tycoon Bhupendra Kansagra, owner of the budget airline, Spicejet. No details have been leaked to the media why that romance had ended.

The South African police are adamant that they have established "without reasonable doubt" that Shrien Dewani, having failed to find a way out of his engagement, had found a "way out" of his marriage. It was murder.

But someone is as adamant that Shrien Dewani is innocent. He is Kamlesh Vyas from the Bristol mosque where Shrien worshiped and who has known him for 10 years. Speaking of Shrien, he told the English media: "You couldn't think of him killing even a fly."

Ashok Hindocha, Anni's uncle, on the contrary, told London's The Daily Mail when referring to how Shrien had not defended Anni: "I would not even have allowed my dog to be left like that. I would fight for the dog. I would never in my life have done that. He could have punched them, he could have done anything to resist."

On Saturday, May 14, Anni's ashes were scattered onto the waters of a lake near Mariestad in Sweden where she was born and grew up. The Hindochas made the Dewanis understand that they were not to attend the ceremony.

Anish Hindocha, Anni's brother, cradled the urn on his lap for the journey by boat out over the lake.

"This is where Anni belongs," said Vinod Hindocha, Anni's father, after the scattering of his daughter's ashes.

But where does Shrien Dewani belong? In a secure mental asylum? In a jail? Or in an office running his family's care home business, a totally innocent man?

On Monday, June 13, as expected, only Qwabe turned up for the scheduled trial. Earlier, the court had received a certificate from Groote Schuur Hospital confirming that Mngeni had undergone surgery to remove the malignant tumor from his brain and was still one of its patients.

Ashok Hindocha, Anni's uncle, had made the long flight from London to Cape Town for the trial. He told reporters: "We would like to thank everyone, including the South African police and judicial system for their support of our family."

None of the Dewanis had made the trip.

Chief Magistrate Jackie Redelinghuis told the court that a Groote Schuur Hospital assessment of Mngeni's condition stated that he would be fit to stand trial within two months.

Redelinghuis then postponed the trial until Tuesday, August 2.

The South African police are confident that on that day Shrien Dewani, having been extradited, would be under lock and key in a Cape Town jail.

However, there was still no trial taking place.

Finally, Tuesday, August 2, arrived, and both the Cape Town police and prosecutors appeared disappointed as two individuals were absent from court. One was Shrien Dewani, and the other was the ailing Xolile Mngeni.

On Tuesday, July 19, during Shrien's rescheduled extradition hearing at Belmarsh Magistrates' Court in London, his lawyers had portrayed him as suicidal and claimed that he would take his own life if extradited. Shrien, visibly unwell and bloated, was present in court. Due to his mental state, the judge decided to postpone the extradition hearing. A new hearing was set for Wednesday, August 10, and Shrien was taken back to the secure unit of Blackberry Hill Hospital near Bristol.

Regarding Xolile Mngeni, despite undergoing surgery and receiving chemotherapy, his brain tumor, known as pineoblastoma, was terminally affecting him. Medical reports presented in court on Tuesday, August 2, indicated that he experienced visual abnormalities and hallucinations. Even if the treatment aimed to eradicate the cancer, he would never be in a "medical state" suitable for answering charges in court. In essence, his treatment was palliative.

Qwabe stood alone in the dock, and his lawyer noted the significant stress caused by the prolonged duration of the case. With the trial for both him and co-accused Mngeni once again postponed, Qwabe was driven back to his jail cell, feeling further amplified stress.

The new trial for the two was scheduled for Tuesday, September 20, although there were doubts that Mngeni would be able to face justice on that date.

However, Anni Dewani's relatives, friends, and the countless individuals from around the world who had become invested in seeking justice for her brutal murder during her honeymoon refused to abandon hope. They held onto the expectation that during Shrien's next extradition hearing on August 10, the judge would rule in favor of his extradition to South Africa.

And on August 10, the judge did just that.

Anni's family and friends sat silently on the hard benches in Court Number Three at Belmarsh Magistrates' Court, listening attentively as District Judge Howard Riddle delivered his statement. After two hours of intense listening in the stifling courtroom and outside on the street, they finally heard the judge's decision. Shrien could indeed be extradited to South Africa. The judge dismissed his lawyers' arguments regarding post-traumatic stress, depression, and potential mental illness as insufficient grounds to prevent extradition. The judge also rejected the lawyers' claim that Shrien, described as "good-looking, youthful, and physically well-preserved," would be targeted by inmates with AIDS. He expressed confidence that Shrien would be held in a single cell within one of South Africa's top prisons.

However, the celebration over the judge's verdict came to an abrupt halt when it was pointed out by the media that the ruling was not final. The ultimate decision rested with Home Secretary Theresa May, and this process could take weeks or even months as she needed to thoroughly review the extensive Dewani dossier. In the

United States, the equivalent authority would be Ken Salazar, the Secretary of the Interior at the Department of the Interior, responsible for internal affairs. Even if May confirmed the judge's verdict, Shrien's lawyers were expected to file an appeal at London's High Court. Furthermore, Shrien would not be extradited for an immediate trial but for questioning by the South African police, who would need to establish beyond reasonable doubt that he had orchestrated his bride's murder before he could be brought to trial.

Meanwhile, as the case continued to drag on, rumors persisted about Shrien's sexuality and Anni's doubts about his virility. Neither of them had wanted to go through with the marriage, but they felt obligated due to the significant amount of money their parents had spent on the wedding.

The rumor of Shrien's homosexuality gained some validation when one of the South African investigators leaked the testimony of Rani Kansagra, a girl whom Shrien had been engaged to before Anni. Rani, now 26 years old and the daughter of wealthy Bhupendra Kansagra, owner of the low-cost airline Spicejet, revealed the reason behind their broken engagement to the South African media. The London tabloids quickly featured the story on their front pages. According to Rani, Shrien had ended their engagement only a few days after it began, explaining that he was sexually impotent and therefore unable to have sexual relations with her.

On Tuesday, September 20, Mngeni, still undergoing treatment for his supposedly incurable brain cancer, entered the court with Qwabe for the scheduled appearance to reassess his fitness to stand trial. However, the outcome mirrored previous appearances, and soon the two friends were back in the police vehicle returning them to their cells. During the appearance, neither Magistrate Jackie Redelinghuis nor Chief Prosecutor Rodney de Kock and his assistant Deputy Prosecutor Adrian Mopp mentioned Mngeni's illness. They declared him fit to stand trial alongside Qwabe.

Although no trial date was set, Magistrate Redelinghuis scheduled a pretrial hearing at the Cape Town High Court for Friday, February 10, 2012. The purpose of the hearing was to confirm Mngeni's fitness to stand trial.

As Mngeni and Qwabe's fate was nearly determined, the Dewani family awaited Home Secretary Theresa May's decision regarding Shrien's extradition to South Africa.

On Monday, September 26, May communicated her decision to Shrien's lawyers and his family, but the news was not released to the media until four days later. May, after careful consideration of all relevant factors, concluded that Shrien would be extradited to South Africa and subsequently signed the extradition order.

However, under British law, an accused individual has the opportunity to appeal an extradition order. Shrien took advantage of this right and wasted no time in doing so.

On Friday, September 30, the English law firm Hickman and Rose lodged an appeal on Shrien's behalf. A spokesperson for the firm stated that their client maintained his innocence and his intention to clear his name from all false allegations. They also claimed that Shrien's health was too precarious for him to return to South Africa, as his condition would deteriorate, and he highlighted the existence of several serious risks to Shrien's life and safety in the country. However, the spokesperson did not specify what these risks were.

It could take two to three months before the appeal could be heard at the British High Court and should Shrien lose it, he could take his case to the Supreme Court, and if the extradition order is again confirmed, then he could take his case to the European Court of Human Rights in Strasbourg, France.

If this is the road Shrien Dewani will choose to take then Anni's family and their on-line supporters who had taken a petition signed by 11,510 angry people to Ms May to request her to extradite Shrien, might have to wait some time still – a couple of years even – for justice.

Shrien wins appeal

On Friday, March 30, Shrien Dewani learned that the British High Court had temporarily halted his extradition to South Africa.

Sir John Thomas, President of the Queen's Bench Division of the High Court, said that although it is "plainly in the interest that Dewani be tried in South Africa" his mental state does not allow him currently to stand trial. Sir John explained that to extradite him to South Africa would be "unjust and oppressive" and that if he remained in Britain there were "increased prospects of a speedier recovery" from his mental problems.

So eager were the South African authorities to have Shrien back in South Africa that they even said that he could serve his sentence in England if found guilty in a Cape Town court of having masterminded his bride's murder. However, a spokesperson for the British Ministry of Justice dismissed the idea by pointing out that no prisoner transfer agreement existed between Britain and South Africa and for that matter with any other country.

Ami Denborg, Anni's sister, told reporters outside the court that her family now wished Shrien a speedy recovery so that he could return to South Africa and "finally tell us what happened because we want to know the truth."

A spokesperson for the Dewani family claimed that the family too wished for Shrien's recovery and said, "He is innocent and is determined to return to South Africa to clear his name and seek justice for his wife Anni."

The Trial

After resisting extradition for three years to South Africa and then deemed mentally fit to stand trial,Dewani was brought to trial in October of 2014. On December 9, 2014 he won acquittal. In setting Dewani free, Judge Jeanette

Traverso of the Western Cape High Court ruled that the prosecution had failed to present any "evidence on which a reasonable court can convict the accused" and that the prosecution's case "cannot pass legal muster."

During trial, the prosecutors claimed Dewani paid 15,000 rand (about $1,300) to have three men kill his wife in a contrived carjacking. They said his motive was that he was gay and had been pressured by his family to marry against his will.

Those three men were previously convicted of Anni Dewani's murder. As part of a plea deal to shorten their sentences, they agreed to testify against Dewani. One of the convicted died before trial, but the other two were the star witnesses for the prosecution. The judge found their testimony "far below" the legal threshold for credible testimony.

Outside the courthouse, the family of the victim expressed outrage at the verdict. Following close on the heels of the lenient verdict given to Oscar Pistorius, the impression that wealthy defendants are immune from justice in South Africa was reinforced.

Case 5

The Life and Times of Clarence Ray Allen

The individual in question was named Clarence Ray Allen. He was born in Blair, Oklahoma in 1930 and claimed to have Choctaw heritage, identifying himself as a member of the Muskhogean Indian tribe, which includes the Creek, Chickasaw, Choctaw, and Seminole tribes.

Allen's family was destitute, and as a result, he grew up working in the cotton fields. However, Allen was ambitious and eventually relocated to Fresno, California. There, he got married and established his own successful security company. With his charisma and hard work, Allen's company thrived, allowing him to progress from renting a modest shack for $75 per month to owning a ranch where he raised prestigious show horses, including Thoroughbreds and Arabians. He also owned an airplane and had a swimming pool in his backyard.

Despite his accomplishments and wealth, Allen was unsatisfied. There was a dissonant aspect to his personality, perhaps due to boredom or some suggested mental instability. Whatever the reason, his mindset became corrupted, and he turned to a life of crime. He formed his own gang, which he named the Ray Allen Gang. Due to his outgoing nature, Allen attracted people easily, including young and impressionable individuals who sought an escape from their dissatisfying lives.

Allen recruited these individuals, providing them with guidance and leading them into a life of crime. The most crucial rule of the Ray Allen Gang was a strict "no snitching" policy, with Allen warning that informants would be killed. To emphasize his point, he presented a newspaper article about two individuals who were found dead in Nevada, stating that snitches received only one punishment.

The gang embarked on a series of meticulously planned robberies, targeting both homes and businesses. Allen orchestrated these robberies, displaying a natural talent for this illicit activity. It seemed to provide him with enjoyment, an easy way to earn money and experience a thrill, all without causing harm to anyone.

However, everything changed in 1974 when Allen decided to rob Fran's Market in Fresno. Not only did he know the store's owners, but they were also his friends. This familiarity made the store an easy target, as Allen possessed detailed knowledge of its layout and security. To carry out the plan, Allen enlisted the help of his son, Roger, Roger's girlfriend, and two other willing accomplices, Carl Mayfield and Lee Furrow.

The plan unfolded as follows: Roger devised a scheme where Bryon Schletewitz, whose parents were Fran's Market owners, would be invited to swim at Ray's house. Bryon would change into his swimsuit, leaving his clothes in a nearby bathhouse. While Bryon was swimming, one of the gang members would search his pockets and steal the store keys. Meanwhile, Mary Sue Kitts, who was Roger's girlfriend, would flirt with Bryon and show interest in him.

The plan worked perfectly. Later that night, Bryon asked Mary Sue out on a date. While Mary Sue kept Bryon occupied, Ray, Roger, and the other gang members used the stolen keys to enter the store and go straight to the safe. They were unable to open it, so they took the entire safe with them. When they managed to open the safe later, they found $500 in cash and $10,000 in money orders. The gang started cashing the stolen money orders in various locations in Southern California without raising suspicion or causing harm.

However, the situation took a turn when Mary Sue felt guilty and everything spiraled out of control. She confessed to Bryon about the theft, including how they stole the keys, took the safe, and cashed the money orders. She even admitted to deceiving Bryon by pretending to like him. Hurt and angry, Bryon confronted Roger and asked if Mary Sue's revelations were true. Roger admitted to the robbery.

After the confrontation with Bryon, Roger informed his father, Ray, about Mary Sue's confession and how Bryon now knew about the store robbery. According to court records, Roger eventually testified against his father and revealed that Ray decided that Mary Sue and Bryon needed to be dealt with.

To prevent any trouble, Ray visited Bryon's parents and lied to them, claiming that he considered Bryon like his own son because of his affection for the boy. Ray then told a significant lie by denying his involvement in the store robbery. However, he later revealed the truth and hinted that if Bryon's parents caused any legal trouble, they might face severe consequences, including rumors of their house being burned down. To reinforce the message, Ray paid someone named Lee Furrow $50 to drive by their house at night and shoot at it.

Ray also decided to eliminate any loose ends, and Mary Sue Kitts was the most problematic loose end. During the gang's next meeting, Ray accused Mary Sue of being a snitch, which was a severe violation of their rules. The gang unanimously voted to sentence Mary Sue to death.

Ray devised a plan to poison Mary Sue. They would invite her to a party held at Shirley Doeckel's apartment, Ray Allen's girlfriend. During the party, Lee Furrow was supposed to offer Mary Sue some pills, claiming that they would all get high together. However, the pills would actually be cyanide. Once Mary Sue died, they would dispose of her body.

However, Lee Furrow and Shirley Doeckel hesitated to go along with the plan. Lee didn't want to kill a young girl, and Shirley didn't want the murder to happen in her apartment. They expressed their concerns to Ray, but Ray convinced Shirley that the murder needed to take place and that the apartment was the best location. Although Lee Furrow still objected, Ray threatened to kill him if he didn't comply, making it clear that two murders were just as easy as one. Feeling trapped, Lee reluctantly agreed.

On the night of the party, Mary Sue had no idea about the impending events or the kind of dangerous individuals she was dealing with. When Mayfield and Furrow offered her the pills, she declined, stating that she preferred to drink wine when she got high, and the party didn't have any. Perplexed about what to do, Mayfield and Furrow contacted Ray, who was growing impatient. Ray instructed them to find a way to carry out the murder, but they were unable to come up with a plan. They called Ray again, and he decided to go to the apartment himself.

Ray met Furrow outside the apartment, frustrated with the lack of progress. He emphasized that he didn't care how it was done but urged Furrow to proceed with the murder.

Ray informed Furrow that unless he completed the assigned task, Ray would kill him. Furrow then returned to the party and later found himself alone with Mary Sue. He forcefully grabbed her and began strangling her. Despite her attempts to resist, Furrow's strength overpowered her. However, their struggle was interrupted by a phone call. Furrow paused his assault to answer the phone, leaving Mary Sue gasping for breath. Ray asked if Furrow had killed her, to which

Furrow replied negatively. Ray angrily instructed him to do so and ended the call.

Following Ray's command, Furrow proceeded to strangle Mary Sue to death. The next objective for the gang was to dispose of her body, and Ray had meticulously planned the process. They took her body to the Friant-Kern canal, where Furrow used a knife to dismember it. They wrapped the remains and attached stones to ensure the body sank. Ray kept watch for passing cars while the gang dropped Mary Sue's body into the canal's dark waters. Her body was never found.

Ray made sure that everyone involved understood their equal guilt in the gruesome event. They were all considered accomplices to murder. The following day, Furrow disappeared, and Mayfield questioned Ray about his whereabouts. Ray falsely claimed that Furrow no longer existed because he had been killed in Mexico for a mere $50. However, Furrow was still alive and would later assist Ray in a jewelry store robbery.

Six months later, Mayfield expressed concerns about potential informants or deals with the authorities. Ray assured him that if anyone were to betray them, they would be dealt with, even if Ray was in prison. He claimed that he would reach out and kill them from behind bars if necessary.

After a period of laying low, Ray grew restless and began planning new robberies. He recruited two new members, Allen Robinson and Benjamin Meyer, but made sure they understood his ruthless approach to dealing with snitches. Ray recounted a previous incident where a woman had become problematic and was killed by the gang. He warned that anyone who betrayed him or his family would face the same fate, regardless of where they tried to hide. Meyer asked what Ray would do if he were in jail and unable to act, to which Ray menacingly replied that his influence extended beyond prison walls.

Ray's new plan involved targeting K-Mart stores, starting with the one in Tulare, California. The gang successfully robbed the Tulare store, securing $16,000. However, Ray believed that Allen Robinson had made mistakes during the heist and contemplated killing him. Instead, he replaced Robinson with Larry Green as a new gang member.

A month later, during their robbery of the Visalia K-Mart store, things took a turn for the worse. Larry Green made a critical error and accidentally shot an innocent bystander. As police arrived at the scene, Green, Meyer, and Ray Allen were arrested. Clarence Ray Allen faced trial and was convicted of robbery, attempted robbery, and assault with a deadly weapon.

With their leader incarcerated, the Ray Allen Gang began to dissolve, and individuals started looking out for themselves. Many gang members testified against Ray Allen in his trial for the murder of Mary Sue Kitts. Lee Furrow made a deal and received a reduced sentence in exchange for his testimony. Other witnesses who testified against Ray included Bryon Schletewitz, Carl Mayfield, Shirley Doeckel, and Ben Meyer.

In his second trial, Clarence Ray Allen was convicted of burglary, conspiracy, and the first-degree murder of Mary Sue Kitts. He received a life sentence without the possibility of parole and was sent to Folsom Prison. While there, he befriended Billy Ray Hamilton, also known as "Country," and Gary Brady, both of whom were soon to be paroled. Ray managed to manipulate them, convincing them to carry out murders on his behalf. He promised Hamilton $25,000 for the killings.

Ray's plan involved his son Kenny providing the necessary money, firearms, and transportation. Once Hamilton was paroled, Kenny would meet up with him and supply him with the required items for the murders. Hamilton's initial targets were the owners of Fran's Market and Bryon Schletewitz, their son.

After Hamilton's release, Kenny met him at the Fresno bus depot, accompanied by Connie Barbo, Hamilton's girlfriend. Barbo had expressed her willingness to participate in the planned murder spree for a sum of money and drugs.

Kenny supplied Hamilton with a modified shotgun, a .32 caliber revolver, and ammunition. Hamilton and his girlfriend drove to Fran's Market in a car provided by Kenny, intending to target Raymond Schletewitz and his son, Bryon Schletewitz. However, upon arriving at the market, they abandoned their plan when they encountered a 15-year-old boy inside and Barbo refused to harm someone so young.

The following night, Hamilton and Barbo returned to Fran's Market. Hamilton brandished the shotgun recklessly, while his girlfriend aimed the .32 caliber pistol at the store employees. There were four employees present, including

Bryon Schletewitz. Hamilton gathered everyone together and instructed his girlfriend to keep watch over them. He then took Bryon to the nearby stockroom and fatally shot him in the head. Upon his return, Hamilton inquired about the location of the store's safe from employee Douglas White, who claimed there was none. In response, Hamilton shot White in the chest, instantly killing him. The sound of the shotgun, coupled with the chaotic violence and blood, caused employee Josephine Rocha to cry uncontrollably. Annoyed by her sobbing, Hamilton shot her in the heart, killing her. He then aimed at the remaining employee, Joe Rios, intending to shoot him in the face. However, Rios managed to raise his arm just in time, resulting in the shotgun blast hitting his elbow instead.

Believing he had eliminated everyone, Hamilton decided it was time to leave since there were no more targets. As Hamilton and Barbo exited the store, they were confronted by Jack Abbott, a neighbor who had been alerted by the sound of the shotgun. Hamilton momentarily halted, but quickly retaliated by firing a shotgun blast in Abbott's direction. Abbott returned fire but missed. While Hamilton and Abbott engaged in a shootout, Barbo sought refuge in the safety of the store's ladies' restroom.

The gunfight between Hamilton and Abbott continued outside. Hamilton wounded Abbott with a shot, but Abbott, despite being injured, still fought back. Abbott fired a shot at Hamilton as he made a dash for his getaway car. The bullet struck Hamilton's foot, but he managed to reach the car and escape.

A short while later, the police arrived at Fran's Market with sirens blaring. Upon entering the store, they discovered a scene resembling a battlefield, with blood and carnage everywhere. Three employees were found dead, and Joe Rios was severely wounded. The police called for an ambulance and conducted a thorough search of the building. They eventually discovered Barbo hiding in a stall in the restroom, where she was promptly arrested.

Meanwhile, Hamilton located a phone and contacted Kenny Allen. According to investigators' reports, Hamilton informed Kenny that he had "lost his kitten" and needed a new car since the police now had a description of the one he was driving. The two men arranged to meet and exchanged cars. Seeking a place to hide, Hamilton headed north to Modesto, where his former prison acquaintance Gary Brady resided. Brady provided him shelter. While staying at Brady's place, Hamilton confessed to Brady that he had killed three people for Ray, as stated in Brady's testimony.

In need of money, Hamilton asked Brady's wife to write a letter to Ray, demanding the $25,000 owed to him for the job. Unfortunately, the letter contained their apartment's address as the return address. While awaiting a response from Ray, Hamilton decided to rob a liquor store across the street from the apartment complex. This ill-advised move led to his arrest by the Modesto Police.

Meanwhile, Kenny Allen faced his own troubles as he was apprehended by the police on drug-related charges. During the investigation, the police connected Kenny to the violent incident at Fran's Market. They interrogated him about the murders, to which he initially denied any involvement. However, a week later, Kenny offered to testify against Hamilton, Barbo, and his father in exchange for protective custody and the ability to choose his prison, fearing retribution from his father.

In June 1981, Clarence Ray Allen was charged with three counts of murder under special circumstances and conspiracy to commit murder. Kenny Allen testified against his father during a preliminary hearing but later decided to change his testimony at the actual trial. This decision nullified the plea bargain, and Kenny Allen was subsequently charged with the three murders at Fran's Market by the district attorney.

After reconsidering once again, Kenny Allen ultimately chose to testify fully and truthfully against his father during the trial. Clarence Ray Allen, against the norm in murder trials, took the stand in an attempt to convince the jury of his innocence. While testifying, Allen denied any involvement in the Fran's Market murders and the conspiracy to kill witnesses who had testified against him. However, he admitted to writing the letters presented as evidence and to transporting and disposing of Mary Sue Kitts' body. He denied any role in her murder.